Extending Dynamics 365 Finance and Operations Apps with Power Platform

Integrate Power Platform solutions to maximize the efficiency of your Finance & Operations projects

Adrià Ariste Santacreu

BIRMINGHAM—MUMBAI

Extending Dynamics 365 Finance and Operations Apps with Power Platform

Group Product Manager: Alok Dhuri

Publishing Product Manager: Kushal Dave

Senior Editor: Esha Banerjee

Technical Editor: Vidhisha Patidar

Copy Editor: Safis Editing

Indexer: Tejal Soni

Production Designer: Nilesh Mohite

DevRel Marketing Coordinator: Deepak Kumar and Mayank Singh

First published: January 2024

Production reference: 1050124

Published by Packt Publishing Ltd.

Grosvenor House

11 St Paul's Square

Birmingham

B3 1RB, UK

ISBN 978-1-80181-159-0

www.packtpub.com

Contributors

About the author

Adrià Ariste Santacreu has been working in the Microsoft Business Applications sphere since 2010, starting with Axapta and Microsoft Dynamics AX, and since 2016 with Microsoft Dynamics 365 F&O. Adrià is a technical solutions architect and developer who loves solving requirements with all the tools available in the Microsoft ecosystem, including Power Platform and the Azure services that can be used with Finance and Operations. Adrià has been recognized as a Microsoft MVP since 2020 in the Business Applications category thanks to his community contributions, including speaking at events and conferences and writing technical articles about Dynamics 365 F&O, Azure, Dataverse, and the Power Platform.

About the reviewers

Cesar Garibaldo is a principal consultant in Microsoft's Industry Solutions Delivery team, with over 13 years of experience implementing D365 F&O and 4 years in D365 CE/Power Platform. With a dual proficiency in both functional areas (Finance, SCM, Sales) and technical roles (Integrations, Data Migration, Development), he has contributed to over 25+ ERP/CRM implementations across 14 industries (Professional Services, Retail, Government) in the US, Canada, and Latin America. Fluent in both English and Spanish, Cesar has successfully delivered projects in both languages. He holds multiple certifications in D365 F&O, CE, and Power Platform.

Nathan Clouse, a Microsoft MVP, is renowned for his expertise in ERP and Microsoft Dynamics Finance and Operations. His career is marked by a passion for developing practical, results-oriented technology solutions that align closely with business objectives. With a robust background in business and accounting, Nathan excels at bridging the gap between technical and business perspectives, ensuring that technology implementations enhance operational efficiency and meet strategic goals. His active role in the technology community highlights his dedication to sharing knowledge and contributing to the advancement of enterprise technology solutions.

I would like to thank my wife and children, the author, and the publishing team.

— *Nathan Clouse*

Table of Contents

Part 2: Extending Dynamics 365 F&O with Power Platform

3

Power Automate Flows in Dynamics 365   43

4

Replacing F&O Processes with Power Automate   61

8

Power BI Reporting for Dynamics 365 F&O Apps   161

Part 3: Adding AI to Your Flows and Apps

9

Integrating AI Builder   183

Part 4: Dataverse and Power Platform ALM

10

Environment Management   211

11

Solution Management   223

Index   245

Other Books You May Enjoy   252

Preface

I have been lucky enough to have been working with Dynamics 365 Finance and Operations since it was released in 2016, when it was first known as AX7. At that time, everything was new for the people who had been working with the previous versions such as Axapta 3.0 or Microsoft Dynamics AX 2009/2012.

During the first months of its life, it went through several name changes and suffix additions and removals, but it was just our old Dynamics AX with a shiny new face. Slowly but steadily, it developed into what it is today.

I remember my first contact with Power Platform as clear as day. It was in 2019 during the Microsoft Business Applications Summit in Atlanta. I attended a session where we followed a hands-on lab in which we used AI Builder. I won't lie and make up a magical story wherein I saw all the potential that Power Platform had, because it wasn't like that.

But I can tell you when that moment was: when we got the virtual tables (called virtual entities at the time) functionality, being able to use F&O data from Power Platform with its native connector, and, above all, all the convergence plans where both Power Platform and Dynamics 365 F&O started to benefit from a more real and reliable integration like the one we have today.

With all these changes, and F&O projects having more of a presence in Power Platform, we as consultants need to learn about it. I think this book can serve as an overview of the tools Power Platform has for F&O, from how we can use and integrate data with dual-write or virtual tables, to creating new functionality outside the Enterprise Resource Planning (ERP) with Power Apps and Power Automate.

As a result, this book is intended to help F&O consultants learn more about Power Platform, as well as Power Platform consultants to learn about some of the different concepts in F&O.

Who this book is for

This book will help consultants specializing in Dynamics 365 Finance and Operations, along with those in the Power Platform field, who are eager to discover how to effectively use various Power Platform tools in their F&O projects.

Technical and solutions architects will find value in acquainting themselves with strategies for addressing business needs using the array of tools provided by Power Platform.

Functional and technical consultants will also benefit from reading this book to learn how we can integrate the data from the ERP and Dataverse and get a general overview of Power Platform.

What this book covers

Chapter 1, Dynamics 365 F&O and Low-Code Development, discusses how development has been done traditionally in F&O and how low-code tools like those in Power Platform can help us speed it up. An overview of Power Platform and Dataverse is also provided.

Chapter 2, Dual-Write and Virtual Tables, shows how we can integrate the data from F&O into Dataverse and the benefits and issues that come with both methods.

Chapter 3, Power Automate Flows in Dynamics 365, provides an overview of Power Automate, its connectors, and the triggers and actions we can have inside a flow. We also compare and learn about the differences between using the Dynamics 365 F&O connector and the Dataverse one with virtual tables in flows.

Chapter 4, Replacing F&O Processes with Power Automate, discusses how we can extend the workflow functionality in F&O using Power Automate and have users approve or reject flows from Teams or emails.

Chapter 5, Building Automations and Integrations, shows how we can use a Power Automate flow instead of X++ to connect to a FTP/SFTP server to retrieve a file and update data inside F&O.

Chapter 6, Power Apps: What's in It for Finance and Operations Consultants, serves as an introduction to Power Apps and how we can embed them in existing F&O forms.

Chapter 7, Extend F&O Apps with Power Apps, shows an example of building a canvas Power App in which we display F&O data, create filters, and update the data back in F&O from the canvas app.

Chapter 8, Power BI reporting for Dynamics 365 F&O Apps, shows how we can export data from F&O into Azure Data Lake Storage thanks to the Synapse Link functionality and virtual tables.

Chapter 9, Integrating AI Builder, introduces us to AI Builder and its custom and pre-trained models, and shows examples of using those models inside a Power App and from Power Automate.

Chapter 10, Environment Management, serves as an introduction to the Power Platform admin center and Dataverse environments.

Chapter 11, Solution Management, serves as an introduction to the Application Lifecycle Management (ALM) concept and shows the differences between managed and unmanaged solutions, along with examining how we can move the components we create between environments.

To get the most out of this book

You need to have basic knowledge of Dynamics 365 F&O and some concepts, such as data entities, along with an understanding of modules such as Accounts payable or Accounts receivable.

Software/hardware covered in the book	Operating system requirements
Dynamics 365 Finance and Operations Apps	Windows, macOS, or Linux
Power Platform	Windows, macOS, or Linux

If you are using the digital version of this book, we advise you to type the code yourself or access the code from the book's GitHub repository (a link is available in the next section). Doing so will help you avoid any potential errors related to the copying and pasting of code.

Download the example code files

You can download the example code files for this book from GitHub at `https://github.com/PacktPublishing/Extending-D365-Finance-and-Operation-apps-with-Power-Platform-`. If there's an update to the code, it will be updated in the GitHub repository.

We also have other code bundles from our rich catalog of books and videos available at `https://github.com/PacktPublishing/`. Check them out!

Conventions used

There are a number of text conventions used throughout this book.

`Code in text`: Indicates code words in text, database table names, folder names, filenames, file extensions, pathnames, dummy URLs, user input, and Twitter handles. Here is an example: "OData actions are special methods executed on data entities that are decorated with the `SysODataAction` attribute."

A block of code is set as follows:

```
Patch(
    'CustomersV3',
    LookUp('CustomersV3', 'Customer account' = CustomerGallery.
Selected.'Customer account'),
    {
        'Credit limit': Value(CreditLimitInput.Text)
    }
);
Refresh(CustomersV3);
Set(CreditLimitValue, Value(CreditLimitInput.Text));
```

When we wish to draw your attention to a particular part of a code block, the relevant lines or items are set in bold:

```
[SysODataAction('AASPostSalesOrder', false)]
    public static str postSalesorder(SalesId _salesId)
    {
        SalesFormLetter salesFormLetter;
        salesTable        salesTable;

        salesTable        = SalesTable::find(_salesId);
        salesFormLetter =
SalesFormLetter::construct(DocumentStatus::Invoice);

        salesFormLetter.update(salesTable, DateTimeUtil::date
(DateTimeUtil::applyTimeZoneOffset(DateTimeUtil::utcNow(),
DateTimeUtil::getCompanyTimeZone())), SalesUpdate::All,
AccountOrder::None, NoYes::No, NoYes::Yes);

        return CustInvoiceJour::findRecId(salesFormLetter.
parmJournalRecord().RecId).InvoiceId;
    }
```

Bold: Indicates a new term, an important word, or words that you see onscreen. For instance, words in menus or dialog boxes appear in **bold**. Here is an example: "If we open the **EntityKey** node under **Keys** we see there's only one field, the **CustomerAccount** one."

> **Tips or important notes**
> Appear like this.

Get in touch

Feedback from our readers is always welcome.

General feedback: If you have questions about any aspect of this book, email us at customercare@packtpub.com and mention the book title in the subject of your message.

Errata: Although we have taken every care to ensure the accuracy of our content, mistakes do happen. If you have found a mistake in this book, we would be grateful if you would report this to us. Please visit www.packtpub.com/support/errata and fill in the form.

Piracy: If you come across any illegal copies of our works in any form on the internet, we would be grateful if you would provide us with the location address or website name. Please contact us at copyright@packt.com with a link to the material.

If you are interested in becoming an author: If there is a topic that you have expertise in and you are interested in either writing or contributing to a book, please visit authors.packtpub.com.

Share Your Thoughts

Once you've read *Extending Dynamics 365 Finance and Operations Apps with Power Platform*, we'd love to hear your thoughts! Scan the QR code below to go straight to the Amazon review page for this book and share your feedback.

https://packt.link/r/1-801-81159-8

Your review is important to us and the tech community and will help us make sure we're delivering excellent quality content.

Download a free PDF copy of this book

Thanks for purchasing this book!

Do you like to read on the go but are unable to carry your print books everywhere?

Is your eBook purchase not compatible with the device of your choice?

Don't worry, now with every Packt book you get a DRM-free PDF version of that book at no cost.

Read anywhere, any place, on any device. Search, copy, and paste code from your favorite technical books directly into your application.

The perks don't stop there, you can get exclusive access to discounts, newsletters, and great free content in your inbox daily

Follow these simple steps to get the benefits:

1. Scan the QR code or visit the link below

https://packt.link/free-ebook/9781801811590

2. Submit your proof of purchase
3. That's it! We'll send your free PDF and other benefits to your email directly

Part 1: Dynamics 365 Finance and Operations and Power Platform

In this part, we'll delve into the principles of low-code and no-code methodologies and their connection to Power Platform. Additionally, we'll explore the main methods for making F&O data available within Dataverse to use it in Power Platform.

This part has the following chapters:

- *Chapter 1, Dynamics 365 F&O and Low-Code Development*
- *Chapter 2, Dual-Write and Virtual Tables*

1
Dynamics 365 F&O and Low-Code Development

System customization in **Dynamics 365 Finance and Operations Apps** has been a developer job since its early days as Axapta. If you needed to change or create new processes for the ERP, you needed a developer. Now, thanks to **Power Platform**, we can accomplish some of these things using a *low-code approach* that can speed up development and also enhance the overall maintainability of F&O. The goal of this chapter is to provide an understanding of Power Platform and how it can help you, learning about Power Apps or Power Automate, and other low-code elements in Power Platform, allowing you to gain insights of this new technology paradigm.

We will explore the following in this chapter:

- Benefits of low-code and no-code
- The foundation of Power Platform – Dataverse
- Components of Power Platform

Benefits of low-code and no-code

If you've been working with Axapta, Dynamics AX, or the latest and current iteration of the product, Dynamics 365 Finance and Operations, you are already familiar with how changing the default behavior of the system when adding new functionality is done. It will probably involve a developer making changes or creating new objects.

And, if you know how the current development and deployment workflow is done, you must be aware that it's a time-consuming process. You need to have developers available, they must make changes or create a new feature, and once it's tested, you need to promote the changes to a sandbox environment and, finally, to your production environment. Deploying to production will require scheduling downtime, which can be inconvenient and must even be planned with enough time depending on your, or your customer's, business.

What can we do to minimize production downtime?

In an ideal world, the answer would be: plan ahead, make a thorough analysis of your requirements, and have a solid testing strategy before releasing something to production. However, bugs are often unavoidable, and changes of requirements do take place, and sometimes you won't test all the scenarios that will appear in the future.

Here is when Power Platform comes in handy to extend the Dynamics 365 F&O functionality. It will be very hard, or impossible in my opinion, to replace all **X++** **developments** with Power Platform. But it's possible to use Power Platform's low-code tools to enhance Finance and Operations.

Introducing Power Platform

Power Platform (see *Figure 1.1*) is a low-code and no-code development platform built on top of **Microsoft Dataverse**, a data platform with a database, security, file-hosting, logging, and many more features that power the different components of Power Platform:

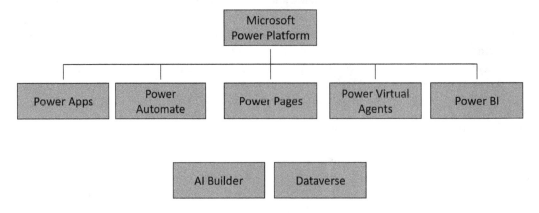

Figure 1.1 – Components of Power Platform

As seen here, Power Platform comprises different low-code tools and components with varying functionalities, enabling you to rapidly develop custom applications, automate processes, or generate insightful reporting, on top of Dataverse.

Understanding low- or no-code

Low-code or no-code is a software development approach that enables us to create applications, websites, or other solutions with little to no programming knowledge. It relies on visual interfaces of the **What You See Is What You Get (WYSIWYG)** type, drag-and-drop components, and templates that allow users to create custom solutions without writing lines of code.

And what are the benefits of low-code tools when using them along Dynamics 365 F&O?

Let's take faster delivery of the customizations as an example. With Power Platform, you won't need to deploy changes to F&O environments. Changing your Power Apps or Power Automate flow will be all you'll need to do. You will also benefit from having more resources in your team to make changes thanks to the way you build solutions in Power Platform: developers' or technical consultants' availability won't be a bottleneck because low-code tools can be easily learned by functional consultants and end users with some training.

Is this the end of X++?

No. And that's not just an opinion, but Microsoft's official stance: "*X++ isn't going anywhere.*" Due to the transactional nature of the ERP and its complex business processes, the most common way of solving the requirements will be through X++ development.

Take the posting of a journal, or a sales order invoice: complex transactional processes that involve different parts of the ERP. If you're willing to extend these processes, you'll have to work with event handlers or a chain of command, like you do nowadays.

At the moment, we can see the business events framework as the most common way of interacting with Power Automate, using it as a trigger. Business events allow us to interact with external systems and send notifications from Finance and Operations.

We also have data events available. Similar to business events, data events trigger when **create, read, update, and delete** (**CRUD**) operations are performed and can be enabled for data entities. These events, thanks to the Power Platform integration, allow us to track changes in data and use them in our Power Apps or Power Automate flows.

Of course, those are not our only ways of interacting with Dataverse solutions, and in this book, we'll learn some others.

> Tip
> With that said, regardless of whether you're an F&O developer or a technical or functional consultant, you should start learning about Power Platform sooner rather than later because it's not Finance and Operations Apps' future; it's already the present!

You will make most of the changes the way you're used to, with the **Application Object Tree** (**AOT**) and X++ in Visual Studio, and thanks to Power Platform, you will add valuable new skills to your toolset. Being able to use Power Automate cloud flows to automate processes, read or write data in Dynamics 365 Finance and Operations, or create a Power App for some users will be a way to reduce coupling from your solutions because it will allow for more agile and faster changes to these processes you're creating.

> Note
> Don't think about Power Platform as a threat to developers but as an additional resource that will make your life easier.

Convergence

With the "*One Dynamics One Platform*" convergence scenario, Microsoft is bringing Dynamics 365 Finance and Operations Apps and Dataverse closer together – improving the experience of integrating both systems and productivity and a more consistent user experience.

We're already benefiting from this! If you remember the early days of **Dual-Write**, we had to configure the environment linking manually. Now, it's possible to deploy a Dataverse environment along a Finance & Operations instance from **Lifecycle Services** (**LCS**) and then configure the integration with Power Platform with only two clicks.

This new LCS experience also helps us configure Dynamics 365 F&O virtual tables in the linked Dataverse environment and use them in our Power Automate flows or Power Apps, instead of using the standard Dynamics 365 F&O connector.

You can see all these investments in Dataverse and F&O from Microsoft go all in the same direction, on the one hand making our life easier with less setup and configuration needs, on the other hand making a more unified Dynamics 365 product line. How many times has a customer asked, "*But isn't everything Dynamics 365?*"?

In the coming years, we will be getting new experiences such as **One Admin**, which will replace LCS for the **Power Platform Admin Center** (**PPAC**). We already have a hint of this because, if you've got Dataverse-linked environments in your projects, you can already see the F&O environment URL in PPAC at the bottom of your environment's page (*Figure 1.2*):

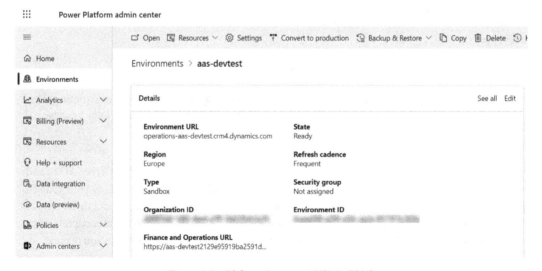

Figure 1.2 – F&O environment URL in PPAC

You can see the Dataverse environment details, with its URL on top under **Environment URL**, and the **Finance and Operations URL** at the bottom.

Another new convergence feature is **One Batch**, which will allow us to have batch jobs in Dataverse, or One Transaction. This will help in providing transactional consistency between Finance and Operations and Dataverse, which have already been announced in the release plans.

The foundation of Power Platform – Dataverse

I've already mentioned Dataverse a few times, and now we're going to learn more about it. First of all, regardless of what we may think upon seeing its name, Dataverse is not a database, which is a common misconception.

Dataverse originated from the **Dynamics CRM** product as the **XRM platform**. In 2018 with the release of Power Apps, its name was changed to **Common Data Service (CDS)**, and after some more name changes, it became the Dataverse we know today.

If not a database... what is a Dataverse?

Dataverse uses relational databases such as **Azure SQL** to store structured data, but it also uses unstructured databases such as **Cosmos DB** for logs, and it also has file storage.

Data and access are secured thanks to security roles to control access to environments, and of course, you can manage users and user groups in your **Azure Active Directory** (**Azure AD**) tenant for authentication. It also has audit capabilities at record levels to know who created, updated, or deleted a record, or also do that at the field level.

Other features include reporting, being able to export data to a data lake, and using **Power BI**, **Business rules** and **Workflows**, or integration capabilities thanks to the API. And of course, you can use **Power Automate** or **Logic Apps** or many Azure services with Dataverse thanks to the Microsoft cloud.

With this short introduction, we agree that Dataverse is not a database. Dataverse is a platform under the SaaS/PaaS model, and all the aforementioned services (see *Figure 1.3*) are transparent to users:

Data and storage
- Relational databases
- Structured and unstructured data
- File storage
- Blob storage

Security
- Authentication
- Auditing
- Security groups
- Logging

Logic
- Jobs
- Workflows
- C# plugins

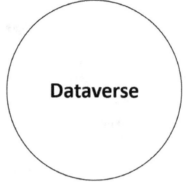

Dataverse

Integration
- API access
- Power automate & Logic apps
- Eventing

Reporting
- Export to Data Lake
- Power BI
- SSRS

Figure 1.3 – Dataverse

We can use PPAC to manage environments, but we will never see the backing services nor have to take care of maintenance, which is also good news! In the background, Dataverse has relational databases, storage, reporting capabilities, and – of course – security, thanks to Azure AD. Having seen the foundation and benefits of Dataverse as the underlying platform, let's explore which elements make up Power Platform itself.

Components of Power Platform

We've already learned about Dataverse, the platform on which Power Platform is built, and now we'll delve into its different components.

Power Apps

Power Apps is probably the most known of Power Platform's products. It is a low-code platform used to create custom applications that can be run on a phone or a tablet thanks to the Power Apps app (see *Figure 1.4*), or a computer using a browser:

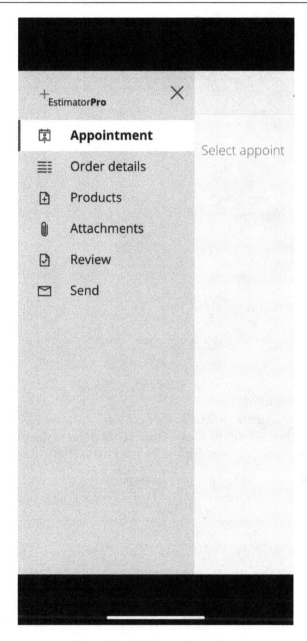

Figure 1.4 – iOS Power Apps player

Thanks to the Power Apps editor we can quickly, and without any programming knowledge, create a canvas app. Thanks to its intuitive UI (see *Figure 1.5*), you can drag and drop the controls you need to the app and customize its design to fit your requirements:

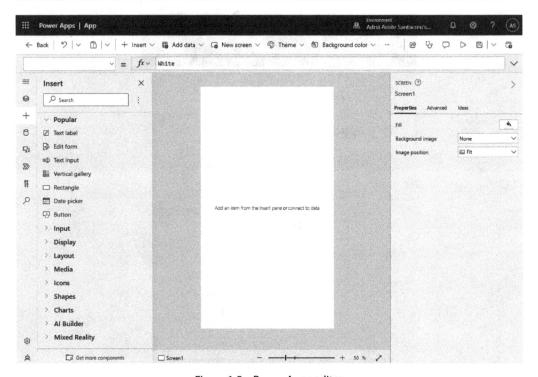

Figure 1.5 – Power Apps editor

You can see this editor is a bit similar to what we have in Visual Studio for F&O. On the left, you can find a toolbox with the different controls, data sources, or components you can add to the app. On the right, you have a **Properties** pane that displays the properties of the selected element.

On top of the design workspace, we find one of the most interesting elements of the UI, an Excel-like formula bar (see *Figure 1.6*). In this bar, we will be able to not only calculate values but also do actions in response to user actions:

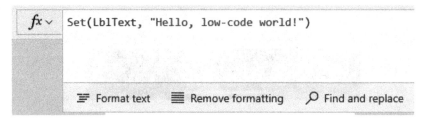

Figure 1.6 – Power Apps formula bar

And of course, we can have a sequence of formulas, so this will look like code. This is one of the places where we'll see most of the code.

Power Automate

The next component we're going to learn about is Power Automate, the automation tool that will enable us to create automations for our business needs. There are two different types of Power Automate flows (see *Figure 1.7*): **cloud flows** that run on the cloud and **desktop flows** that run locally on a Windows PC:

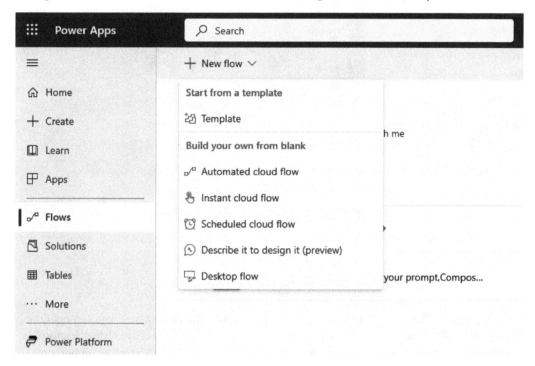

Figure 1.7 – Power Automate flows

In the **Power Apps** maker portal, you can navigate to the **Flows** menu and create a new flow; in our case, a cloud flow. Inside **Cloud flows**, we can choose between:

- **Automated flows**: These will be started when the trigger condition is met

- **Instant flows**: These will be triggered manually; for example, from a button in the Flow app

- **Scheduled flows**: These flows run on a schedule, and you can select their recurrence from minutes to hours, days, or weeks

Designing a flow is quite straightforward using the Power Automate designer, thanks to its intuitive way of creating a flow, using boxes for each step that allow us to pass values between steps and creating complex workflows to automate any process you can imagine (see *Figure 1.8*):

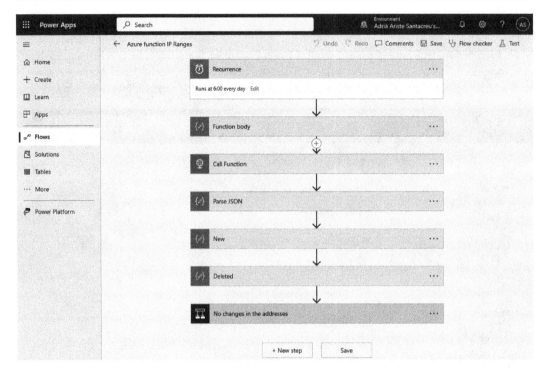

Figure 1.8 – Power Automate scheduled flow

Power Automate is not a standalone complement to Power Platform. For example, you can call flows from a Power App! In that case, the Power App is the trigger, and once the flow has finished, it's possible for the flow to return a value and use that from the Power App, or a Power Virtual Agent bot too.

Power BI

Power BI is probably the oldest member of Power Platform as it's been around for over a decade! That's twice as long as the existence of Power Platform. Probably most of you know Power BI from the existing dashboards (see *Figure 1.9*) in the Dynamics 365 Finance and Operations workspaces, such as the ones in the financial analysis workspace:

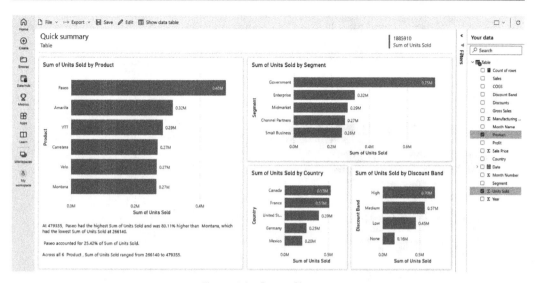

Figure 1.9 – Power BI report

But Power BI is much more than just a reporting tool. It's a **business intelligence** (**BI**) tool that can connect to quite a large variety of data sources such as data lakes, files (*Excel, CSV, JSON*, and so on), *SQL Server*, and even *OData* feeds. And not only to Microsoft products and services but also to other third parties such as *Amazon cloud products, SAP, Oracle, MySQL* databases, and many more (see *Figure 1.10*):

Get Data

Search	**All**
All	IBM Netezza
File	MySQL database
Database	PostgreSQL database
Power Platform	Sybase database
Azure	Teradata database
Online Services	SAP HANA database
Other	SAP Business Warehouse Application Server
	SAP Business Warehouse Message Server
	Amazon Redshift
	Impala
	Google BigQuery
	Google BigQuery (Azure AD) (Beta)
	Vertica
	Snowflake
	Essbase
	Azure SQL database

Certified Connectors | Template Apps   Connect | Cancel

Figure 1.10 – Power BI data sources

It also offers several data-focused tools such as Data Transform and Clean (ETL-ELT) where you can combine data from the different sources you have in the report, and later model it. And finally, it creates stunning visualizations thanks to the different ways of displaying data in graphics (see *Figure 1.11*):

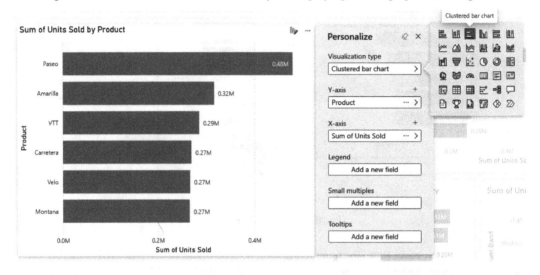

Figure 1.11 – Visualization types

AI Builder

Power Platform also benefits from the latest AI investments made by Microsoft in OpenAI, such as the GPT models. **AI Builder** isn't a standalone component but more like a complement to the other tools in Power Platform. It provides AI models that you can not only use in Power Apps or Power Automate but also in *Teams* or *SharePoint*. As with Power Apps or Power Automate, it can be used without the need for coding skills!

You can build your own AI models, or you can choose one of the many prebuilt models that are ready to use (see *Figure 1.12*):

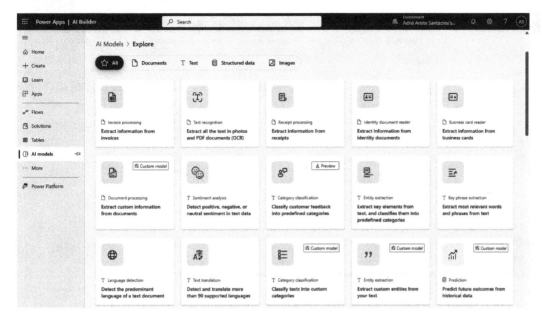

Figure 1.12 – AI Builder prebuilt models

AI Builder is built on Dataverse, which makes the data readily available and prepared for immediate use. This means that if you're using *Dual-Write* or have enabled *F&O virtual tables*, you can use that data with AI Builder without any more work required.

Thanks to the prebuilt models, you can start creating your solutions using invoice processing, receipt processing, or text recognition models to work along F&O from day one. Or, if you need a custom model, you can create one that fits your needs and train it.

Power Pages

Another of the components is Power Pages. Power Pages is a low-code tool used to create websites. It has the same WYSIWYG concept we can find with Power Apps, and you can also use most of the components of Power Platform with it.

This won't be covered in this book, but you can learn more by following the link in the *Further reading* section at the end of this chapter.

PPAC

In PPAC, we can manage the different Dataverse environments (see *Figure 1.13*) we have in our tenant. It's one of the key points regarding Dataverse governance. Here, you'll be able to back up and restore environments and also create new ones for your team:

Figure 1.13 – PPAC environments

It will also be the place where we can give access and assign roles to users in different Dataverse environments. In PPAC, we can also get information on current database and file usage for all our environments, access to other admin centers such as Microsoft 365 or Azure AD, or define **data loss prevention** (**DLP**) policies, among others.

Summary

In this chapter, we learned what low-code and no-code tools are. Then, we dived into Microsoft's own low-code platform – Power Platform – and we looked into how it has introduced new ways of speeding development and enhancing maintainability in F&O.

We had an overview of Microsoft Dataverse, the platform on which Power Platform is built, and where it comes from. We also looked at the convergence plan, which will bring Dynamics 365 Finance and Operations Apps and Power Platform closer together, improving the integration experience and creating a more consistent user experience.

Finally, we learned a bit about the different tools in Power Platform: Power Apps, Power Automate, Power BI, and AI Builder, which can be used alongside Dynamics 365 F&O without replacing X++ development.

In the next chapter, we will look into Dual-Write and F&O Virtual tables. One of the primary functions of these tools is to get our Finance and Operations data out of the box into Dataverse to start working with Power Platform.

Questions

Here are some questions to test your understanding of the chapter. The answers to the questions are given at the end.

1. Used along with Dynamics 365 Finance and Operations, what is the main advantage of low-code tools from Power Platform?

    a. Replacing all X++ developments

    b. Faster delivery of customizations

    c. Eliminating the need for developers

    d. Replacing Dynamics 365 F&O completely

2. What is Power Platform built on top of?

    a. Microsoft Access

    b. Microsoft Dynamics CRM

    c. Microsoft Dataverse

    d. Microsoft SQL Server

3. Which Power Platform component is used for creating low-code custom applications?

    a. Power BI

    b. Power Automate

    c. Power Apps

    d. AI Builder

4. What does Power Automate allow you to do?

    a. Create chatbots

    b. Build custom applications

    c. Create BI reports

    d. Automate processes

5. What is the primary purpose of Microsoft Dataverse in the context of Power Platform and Dynamics 365 Finance & Operations?

    a. It acts as a relational database for storing all Dynamics 365 F&O data.

    b. Dataverse is primarily a development tool for creating custom Dynamics 365 F&O applications.

    c. It is a data platform underpinning Power Platform, providing database, security, file-hosting, and other services.

    d. Dataverse is used exclusively for managing user access and security in Dynamics 365 F&O.

Further reading

If you want to learn more about Dataverse, the Power Platform or low-code you can visit these links:

Official *Microsoft Learn* documentation for Dataverse: `https://learn.microsoft.com/en-us/power-apps/maker/data-platform/`

Official *Microsoft Learn* documentation for Power Platform: `https://learn.microsoft.com/en-us/power-platform/`

What is Low-Code Development?: `https://powerapps.microsoft.com/en-us/what-is-low-code/`

What is Power Pages?: `https://learn.microsoft.com/en-us/power-pages/introduction`

Answers

The following are the answers to the preceding questions:

1. b. Faster delivery of customizations
2. c. Microsoft Dataverse
3. c. Power Apps
4. d. Automate processes
5. c. It is a data platform underpinning Power Platform, providing database, security, file-hosting, and other services.

2
Dual-Write and Virtual Tables

Dynamics 365 Finance and Operations Apps can be integrated with Dataverse and the Power Platform quite easily. Dual-write and virtual tables (formerly virtual entities) will be the primary ways of getting data into Dataverse (Dual-write) or making it readable in Dataverse (virtual entities). The goal of this chapter is to learn about Dual-write and virtual tables, how the finance and operations environment is linked to a Dataverse environment, and which business scenarios we can solve with them. With these features, you'll be able to integrate with Dataverse more easily and use some of the Power Platform tools faster.

We will explore the following in this chapter:

- F&O and Dataverse environment linking
- Scenarios for Dual-write
- Scenarios for virtual tables

Technical requirements

To follow what is explained in this chapter, you'll need the following:

- 1 GB of Dataverse capacity available to provision a new environment.
- Access to a **Lifecycle Services** (**LCS**) project with at least the capability to deploy a Tier 1 cloud-hosted environment in your Azure subscription. An available slot to deploy a Tier 2+ sandbox environment is also an option.
- If your tenant doesn't allow everyone to create a Microsoft Power Platform environment, you need to be assigned the Dynamics 365 Administrator or Power Platform Administrator roles in your Active Directory.
- The user that does the setup needs to be licensed with either a Dynamics 365 Finance or Dynamics 365 Supply Chain Management license.

F&O and Dataverse environment linking

Before starting to work with Dual-write or virtual tables, we must have a Finance and Operations environment linked to a Dataverse environment. This is done through the setup of the Power Platform integration.

This was a step that had to be done completely manually in the past. For example, for Dual-write, you had to create application users on Dataverse, create other application users in Finance and Operations, and finally configure the Dual-write environment – linking in the F&O user interface. This was the same for virtual tables. You needed to install the Finance and Operations Virtual Entity solution manually before being able to start using them.

> **Dataverse solutions**
>
> In Dataverse, a solution refers to how different components are grouped. Think of it as a Visual Studio solution, but instead of grouping the new or extended elements in the AOT, it groups Power Automate flows, connections, Power Apps, etc.

Fortunately for us, Microsoft is investing a lot of resources in the Convergence plan, and automating these kinds of things, makes environment linking a streamlined process that is done with just a few button clicks.

In *Chapter 1*, we learned about LCS and the Power Platform Admin Centre (PPAC). These are the tools we'll use to link an F&O environment and a Dataverse environment; more specifically, we use LCS to do the linking and LCS to see additional link information and the Dataverse capacity reports.

> **Plan carefully!**
>
> The linking of a Dataverse and Finance and Operations environment is irreversible. This means once it's done, you will neither be able to change the link to a different Dataverse environment nor remove the Power Platform integration. If you want to remove or change the integration, you need to redeploy the F&O environment.

Configuring the Power Platform integration

There are two ways of configuring the Power Platform integration for F&O environments. The first one is during the environment deployment in LCS (see *Figure 2.1*):

Deployment settings

Visual Studio Customization	>	
Supported version	>	
Customize SQL Database Configuration	>	
Disk space configuration	>	
Premium Storage Settings	>	
Managed Disk Settings	>	
Customize virtual machine names	>	
Power Platform Integration	>	
Dynamics 365 for Finance and Operations	>	
Customize virtual network	>	

Configure Power Platform Environment

⬤◯ Yes

Power Platform template

Dynamics 365 stand... ∨

Environment Type

Sandbox ∨

I agree by selecting the template 'Dynamics 365 standard' that this Finance and Operations environment will be connected to a Power Platform environment with Dataverse. Platform solutions for Dual-write and Virtual Entities will also be installed but not enabled. Data will not be written via Dual-write to the Power Platform environment by default, but can be configured to do so as part of a later step.

By selecting any template other than the one mentioned above, data will be synchronized via Dual-write functionality by default.

The available template options vary based on the licenses for the tenant which owns this LCS project.

☑ Agree

Done

Figure 2.1 – Power platform integration at deployment time

In the **Advanced** option of the environment deployment, you can go to the **Power Platform Integration** tab to configure a Power Platform environment. Then, you can select from the template list in *Figure 2.2*:

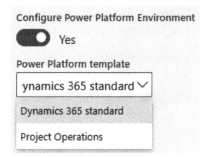

Figure 2.2 – Template selection

The following are the available templates:

- **Dynamics 365 standard**: This template will install the Dataverse solutions for virtual tables and Dual-write and prepare the components for business events

- **Dynamics 365 standard with Dual-write**: This template has the same components as the Dynamics 365 standard one, but it also prepares Dual-write to be configured

- **Project Operations**: This template is used to deploy an F&O environment that will be used with the **Project Operations** solution.

Additionally, you can select the type of Dataverse environment: sandbox or subscription trial (see *Figure 2.3*):

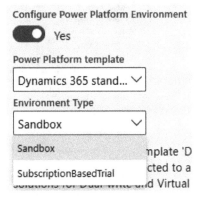

Figure 2.3 – Environment type selection

The sandbox environment is a non-production environment used to develop and test changes. The subscription-based trial is a kind of trial environment but without the 30-day limit that the regular trial environments have. It has a license limit of 25 seats. Select the environment type based on your company's policies.

After completing the setup, the automation creates a new environment in Dataverse and links it to the F&O one you're creating.

These steps are still good for cloud-hosted environments such as the developer boxes. However, this will be deprecated and disabled for new sandbox or production environments (see *Figure 2.4*):

Deployment settings (Finance and Operations - Sandbox (10.0.33 with PU57))

✓ General	**Configure Power Platform Environment**
	◉ No
✓ Change selected topology	Power Platform Integration setup has moved. It is no longer advised to configure it here for Sandbox or Production environments.
✓ Customize SQL Datasets	
✓ Customize solution assets	Enabling Power Platform Integration is now available after the environment is deployed, where you can choose to deploy a new Dataverse instance using a template, or can connect to an existing Power Platform environment that you have deployed previously. Note: all Sandbox and Production environments will be connected at first to a Power Platform environment without Dataverse.
✓ Power Platform Integration	
⚠ Environment notifications	For more information, visit https://aka.ms/ppi-initial-environment
⚠ Environment administrator	☐ Agree
⚠ Summary	
⚠ Customer sign off	

Figure 2.4 – Sandbox or production Power Platform integration is not possible

If you try doing it in one of those environment types, when you get to the **Power Platform Integration** tab, you will see a message telling you that's not possible anymore and the checkbox will be disabled. We will then have to go the second way.

> Tip
> If you need to configure the Power Platform integration in a one-box environment, the ones deployed in your or your customer's subscription this is the only way of doing it. If you deploy it without configuring the integration, you won't be able to do it later.

The second way of configuring the integration is doing it after the environment has been provisioned and is ready. Open the selected environment's LCS details page and scroll down to the **Power Platform Integration** section where you will find a **Setup** button. After clicking it, you will see a dialog similar to when you deploy the environment (see *Figure 2.5*):

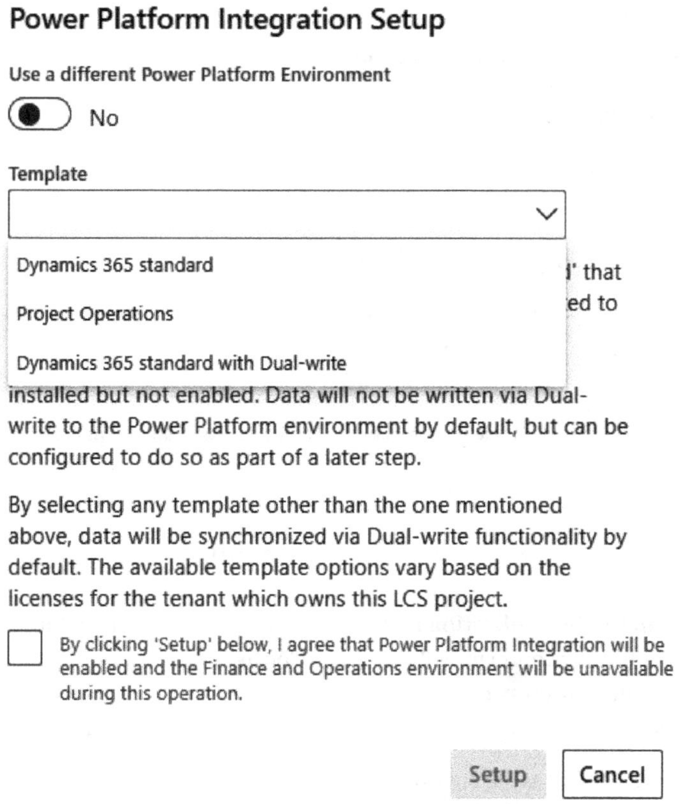

Power Platform Integration Setup

Use a different Power Platform Environment

⚪ No

Template

Dynamics 365 standard		' that
Project Operations		ed to
Dynamics 365 standard with Dual-write	

installed but not enabled. Data will not be written via Dual-write to the Power Platform environment by default, but can be configured to do so as part of a later step.

By selecting any template other than the one mentioned above, data will be synchronized via Dual-write functionality by default. The available template options vary based on the licenses for the tenant which owns this LCS project.

☐ By clicking 'Setup' below, I agree that Power Platform Integration will be enabled and the Finance and Operations environment will be unavaliable during this operation.

Setup   Cancel

Figure 2.5 – Sandbox Power Platform Setup

Here, you need to select one of the available templates and proceed with the setup.

> **Already have a Dataverse environment?**
>
> Notice the **Use a different Power Platform Environment** checkbox? If you select that, you can enter an environment ID from PPAC and it will link it to that existing environment. This is also an operation that can't be undone.

Once the process ends, which takes 60–90 minutes, the status of the LCS environment page will change and you'll be able to set up Dual-write (see *Figure 2.6*):

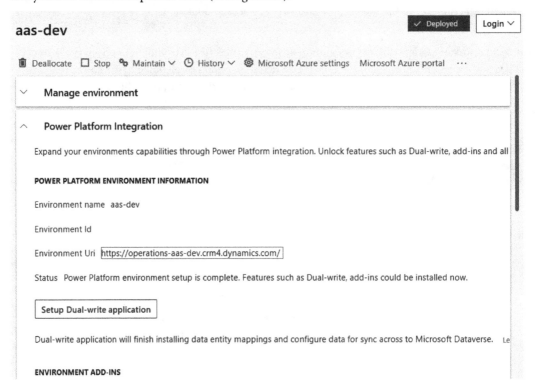

Figure 2.6. Dual-write setup on LCS

Clicking the **Setup Dual-write application** button will display a dialog asking for confirmation, and after that, the status of the environment will change to **Configuring Dual-write application**. When the operation is done, our environment will be linked to Dataverse, and Dual-write and virtual tables will be ready to be used.

Finally, you need to be logged in as the environment administrator in LCS and click the **Link to Power Platform environment** button on LCS to complete the linking. This will leave the environment in a ready state to start running Dual-write.

If the environment where you've configured the integration is a sandbox or production environment, there's an additional **Environment add-ins** section below **Power Platform environment information** (see *Figure 2.7*):

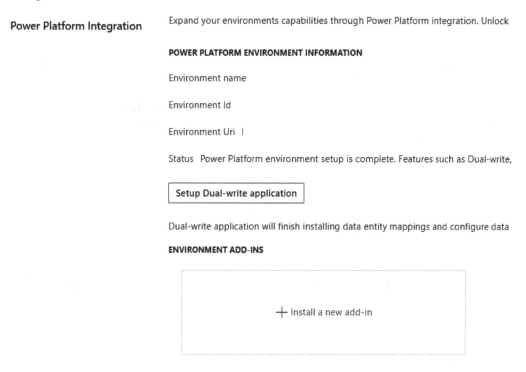

Power Platform Integration

Expand your environments capabilities through Power Platform integration. Unlock

POWER PLATFORM ENVIRONMENT INFORMATION

Environment name

Environment Id

Environment Uri |

Status   Power Platform environment setup is complete. Features such as Dual-write,

Setup Dual-write application

Dual-write application will finish installing data entity mappings and configure data

ENVIRONMENT ADD-INS

+ Install a new add-in

Figure 2.7 – Environment add-ins

If you select the **Install a new add-in** option, you'll be able to enable some of the Dynamics 365 F&O microservices that are installed partially on Dataverse, such as the **Export to Data Lake**, **Finance Insights**, or **Inventory Visibility** add-ins. These are extensions of F&O that host part of their functions on Dataverse.

Dual-write or virtual tables?

Before delving into Dual-write and virtual tables, there is a question you need to ask yourself – do we need to have the data duplicated in both systems? If the answer is no, there's a high probability that you should be using virtual tables; otherwise, you must use Dual-write.

> **Licensing**
> Choosing between Dual-write and virtual tables also has license implications. When using virtual tables, you need to have a Dynamics 365 Finance and Operations license, whereas using Dual-write only requires you to have a license for the system you're accessing.

Let's look into the different features and functionality of both solutions, which will help us answer this question and decide what is best for our needs!

Scenarios for Dual-write

Dual-write is an out-of-the-box integration between Dynamics 365 F&O and the Dynamics 365 customer engagement apps. It is a synchronous and real-time integration that will duplicate data from the ERP to the CRM, from the CRM to the ERP, or in both directions.

It's a tightly coupled solution. This means that there is a close and interdependent relationship between the data in the Finance and Operations apps and the Dataverse apps. For example, if you configure the bidirectional flow between apps, when you make any change in one of the apps, it will be reflected automatically on the other side.

Some of the most important features of the Dual-write infrastructure are as follows:

- Synchronous and near real-time

- Unidirectional (ERP to CRM or CRM to ERP) or bidirectional synchronization

- Out-of-the-box table mappings

- Initial data synchronization – with the initial sync function, we can select a master source (F&O or Dataverse) and the data on that system will be copied onto the other before running the table map

- Table mappings based on F&O data entities

- Extensibility and customization, meaning it's possible to modify existing table maps or create new ones

- Online and offline modes – if any of the apps are offline, changes will be synchronized when they're back online

Now let's learn about Dual-write table mappings and some problems we can solve with them.

Table mappings

Table mappings are the basic building blocks on which Dual-write relies. When your environment is ready to start using Dual-write and go to the Dual-write workspace, you'll probably see no table maps (see *Figure 2.8*):

Figure 2.8 – Dual-write workspace with no table maps

The Dual-write maps are not automatically added if you select the template **Dynamics 365 standard**, but we can add them quickly thanks to the Dataverse solutions that contain the maps (see *Figure 2.9*).

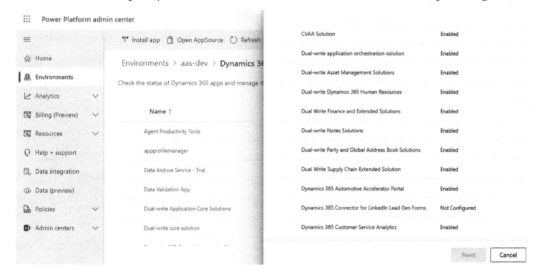

Figure 2.9 – Dual-write solutions in the PPAC

In the PPAC, you can go to the environment details and install the apps that you need. The following are the different Dataverse apps for the different finance and operations apps:

- **Dual-write Application Core**: This lets users install and configure Dual-write without any CRM app. It's a dependency of all the other apps.

- **Dual-write Human Resources**: This contains the solutions needed to sync with the standalone Human Resources Dataverse app.

- **Dual-write Supply Chain**: This has solutions for the supply chain management data.

- **Dual-write Finance**: This includes solutions to synchronize finance data.

- **Dual-write Notes**: This includes solutions to synchronize document attachments from customers, vendors, sales, and purchase orders.

- **Dual-write Asset Management**: This has the solutions needed to share data related to assets and used, for example, with Dynamics 365 Field Service.

- **Dual-write Party and Global Address Book**: This provides solutions used to sync party and global address book data.

> **Note**
>
> To find out more about what each solution contains, you can visit the Microsoft Learn page for Dual-write solutions.
>
> This is a quick-changing document to which maps can be added or changed with each release:
>
> `https://learn.microsoft.com/en-us/dynamics365/fin-ops-core/dev-itpro/data-entities/dual-write/separated-solutions`

So, let's apply a solution to Dual-write and see what happens. In your Dual-write workspace, once you click the Apply solution button, a dialog will open, and it will show the solutions you've installed on your Dataverse environment (see *Figure 2.10*):

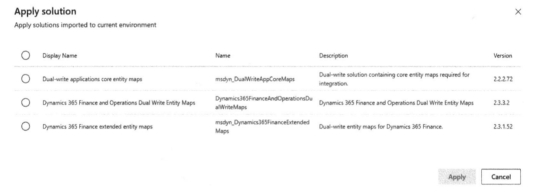

Figure 2.10 – Dual-write table map solutions

In this dialog, you can select as many solutions as you need, and also see the version number in case the solutions have been updated from PPAC. Some of these table mapping solutions include repeated table maps, such as Customers V3 in the finance and supply chain solutions. If you apply a solution that has already been applied to your environment, keep the following in mind:

- If you don't have customized maps, standard maps will be updated if the solution version is newer.

- If you do have customized maps, the maps you've modified won't be updated. You will keep that version and be able to change to the newly installed version.

Once we do this, we will be able to view the available table maps. I will choose the **Customers V3 (accounts)** map to explain a bit more about them (see *Figure 2.11*):

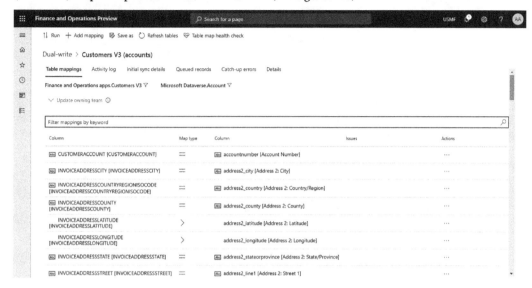

Figure 2.11 – Table mapping screen

A table map is just a finance and operations data entity mapped to a Dataverse table. In this case, the Customer V3 entity is mapped to the Account table. Then, there is a list of fields that are matched between F&O and Dataverse. The map type defines the direction of the synchronization (see *Figure 2.12*):

= bidirectional, when data is changed in the ERP it's updated in the CRM and vice versa.

⤫ same as bidirectional but with transforms.

> from F&O to Dataverse.

▶ from F&O to Dataverse with transforms.

< from Dataverse to F&O.

◀ from Dataverse to F&O with transforms.

Figure 2.12 – Table mapping directions

You can synchronize data bidirectionally, from F&O to Dataverse, or from Dataverse to F&O. Additionally, you can add transforms to all types of table mappings.

This might seem quite easy to understand. However, you might be wondering what transforms are. **Transforms** are a way of mapping fixed values from the CRM to the ERP (see *Figure 2.13*):

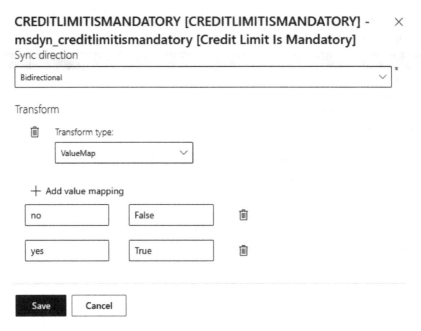

Figure 2.13 – Bidirectional transform

Transforms are especially helpful for enums in F&O. For example, *NoYes enum transform* maps the no value in F&O to false in Dataverse and the yes to true. There are three types of transforms:

- **ValueMap**: Similar to the one in *Figure 2.12*, it maps fixed values from F&O to Dataverse.
- **Default**: This assigns a single value to the field.
- **Truncate**: This is used to truncate the value to the length you specify.

Finally, we can run our table mapping by pressing the **Run** button. Some table maps have prerequisites, such as the customer group table that needs the payment schedule, payment days, and terms of payment to be running. We should also ensure that the legal entities table map should be allowed to run before any other map.

Different concepts between apps

One of the challenges of using Dual-write is getting the ERP and CRM teams to understand concepts that don't exist in their realms. For instance, the company concept doesn't exist in Dataverse, but it's vital for F&O or data entities such as the ERP CustCustomerV3Entity that contains customer data or the VendVendorV2Entity for the vendor data, which are two separate data structures. Both customers and vendors go into the same table in Dataverse: accounts.

Microsoft has solved this with different solutions in both the CRM and ERP, such as adding the company concept to Dataverse or creating a global address book Dataverse solution to synchronize multiple contacts for a vendor or customer between the ERP and CRM. But there's something that you'll have to solve: making both teams speak the same language!

When should I use Dual-write?

Let's look into some examples of when to use Dual-write. Keep in mind the most important features of Dual-write – duplicating data and real-time synchronization. This is really important to remember because once it's enabled and you create, update, or delete a record that has mapping enabled, there will be validations taking place in both the ERP and Dataverse/CRM.

This means that if you, for example, enable the customer group table mapping and create a new customer group in finance and operations, validations will also happen in Dataverse and the record creation will fail if those validations fail as well. The same will happen in the other direction, and believe me, there are many more validations in the ERP than in Dataverse!

> **Why should we use Dual-write?**
>
> The first reason to use Dual-write is to maintain data consistency across your Dynamics 365 products. This is just my opinion, but in your master data management strategy, finance and operations should be the master where data is created and maintained. Dual-write also helps reduce errors. If you rely on processes that involve manually copying data from Dataverse to the ERP, you can incur errors. Thanks to the built-in ERP and CRM validations, Dual-write will help reduce errors and speed up data-copying processes while keeping the data consistent across systems.

The following are some other scenarios where Dual-write can be useful:

- **Customer/vendor data synchronization**: As I already explained with the MDM strategy, Dual-write helps maintain accurate and up-to-date customer/vendor information across all applications. When customer or vendor information is updated in any of the CRM apps, the changes are instantly reflected in Dynamics 365 F&O, ensuring consistent data for billing, shipping, and other processes.

- **Sales orders integration**: When a sales representative creates a sales order in Dynamics 365 Sales, Dual-write makes sure that the sales order information is synced to Dynamics 365 F&O, allowing the team to process and fulfill the order without any delays or manual data entry.

- **Product management**: If your business uses the inventory management capabilities in Dynamics 365 F&O, Dual-write can synchronize this data to Dataverse to ensure sales teams have access to accurate product details, pricing, and inventory on-hand status.

- **Field service integration**: Dual-write can be used to synchronize work order and service-related data between Dynamics 365 Field Service and Dynamics 365 F&O.

- **Project management**: If your organization uses Dynamics 365 Project Operations, Dual-write can synchronize project data, including budgets, resources, and progress updates, between ProjOps and Dynamics 365 F&O.

> **Warning!**
> Don't use Dual Dual-write's initial sync functionality as a data migration tool. It's not what it's meant for, and it has some limitations that discourage the process of migration using initial sync. It's fine to use this functionality to synchronize some master data, but if you want to do a full migration, use something such as the data management framework for F&O.

Scenarios for virtual tables

We've learned about Dual-write, one of the native ways to integrate F&O data with Dataverse. Now it's time to learn about **virtual tables**, earlier known as virtual entities. virtual tables are a Dataverse concept that's not exclusive to F&O. It's a virtual data source that can display data from several different sources in Dataverse.

The most important feature of virtual tables is that the data is not present in Dataverse; we only see a representation of the data from the external system in Dataverse. In the case of Dynamics 365 F&O, we will be able to consume data from the public virtual entities in F&O from Dataverse, but the data will be kept in F&O.

Does this mean we can only read data using virtual tables? No! We can perform all **CRUD** operations and more:

- **Create**: For creating data

- **Update**: For modifying data

- **Delete**: For deleting records

- **Retrieve**: For querying a table with just the columns that you specify in the request

- **RetrieveMultiple**: For retrieving a collection of records to which you pass a query defining which ones to get

- **PerformAction**: For calling OData actions, such as the ones on F&O's data entities decorated with the attribute SysODataAction

Thanks to this, we can use the virtual tables as our data sources in Power Automate, Power Apps, Power Pages, or Power Virtual Agents. And that's not all! Using the data events in F&O, we can use the Dataverse connector in Power Automate as the trigger when creating, updating, or deleting a record.

Enabling virtual tables

Similar to Dual-write, we still need some manual setup to enable virtual tables—regardless of configuring the Power Platform integration – while deploying an environment or after deployment. Furthermore, if you don't have much experience in the CRM side, it can be a bit confusing.

Go to the PPAC and select your environment in the **Environments** tab. Then, click **Settings** (see *Figure 2.14*):

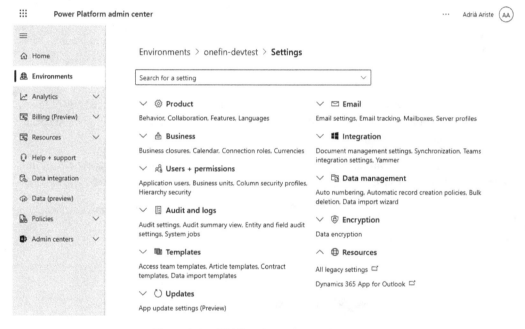

Figure 2.14 – PPAC environment settings page

You will see several sub-menus to manage your environment, but we need to focus on just one. Open the **Resources** sub-menu and select the **All legacy settings** option. This will open one of the old and classic **Dynamics 365** CRM pages (see *Figure 2.15*):

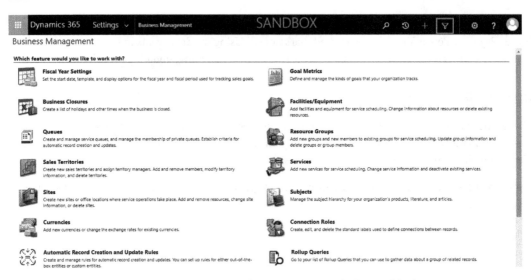

Figure 2.15 – Dynamics 365 legacy settings and advanced find

Although in the **Dynamics 365** settings screen you will see many options, we don't need any of them. Instead, we have to choose the **Advanced Fine** option and click the funnel icon in the top-right corner to open the **Advanced Find** form.

In the **Look for** field, select **Available Finance and Operations Entities**. Then, click on the **Select** link below to add a filter; otherwise, you'll get a list of the over 3,000 available entities (see *Figure 2.16*):

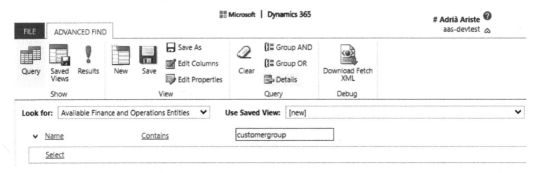

Figure 2.16 – Advanced find with the customergroup filter

In the name field, change the filter to **Contains** and the filter on the customergroup text, as we will enable the virtual table for the customer groups.

> **Tables… or entities?**
>
> You might've already noticed there are some places where virtual tables are referred to as virtual entities. In the past, this was its name. Even today, what are known as tables on the Power Platform maker portal used to be called entities. Of course, this is not to be confused with F&O's data entities; those are still entities and are an entirely different thing!

In the entity list, look for the `CustCustomerGroupEntity` entity and click on the name. A new window with all the fields for that record will open (see *Figure 2.17*):

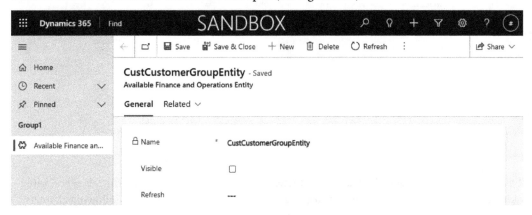

Figure 2.17 – Virtual table fields

To enable the entity as a virtual table, you need to mark the **Visible** checkbox and save the changes. The refresh field is used when there are changes in the F&O data entity. In the case of a new field, for example, you need to select the **Refresh** field and save the changes. The entity definition will be synchronized in Dataverse from F&O.

Likewise, you can unmark the **Visible** checkbox to disable a virtual table.

Once you save, go back to the maker portal and go to the **Tables** section. Change to the **All** filter at the top and look for `mserp` (see *Figure 2.18*):

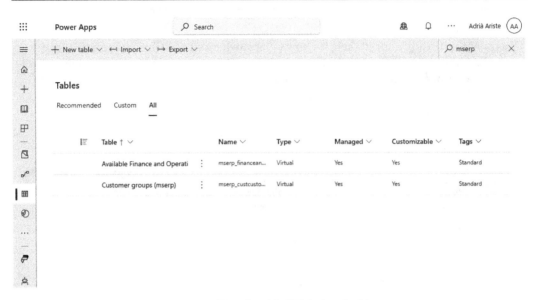

Figure 2.18. List of enabled F&O virtual tables

All the enabled F&O virtual tables will appear there. They have the `mserp` prefix, which is useful while looking for the virtual tables in Power Automate. We will see more of this in the following chapters. Now we're able to use the customer group virtual table.

I have to say I fell in love with F&O virtual tables the first time I tried them. I enabled one of the on-hand virtual tables and created a simple Power App with a grid showing the items and the currently available quantities. For me, that was game-changing, so I may be slightly biased toward virtual tables compared to Dual-write.

When to use virtual tables

Virtual tables are the perfect replacement for the old F&O connector on Dataverse thanks to their CRUD capabilities and ability to use the native connector.

So if you don't need to synchronize data from F&O and Dataverse, virtual tables are the right solution for you. They will enable you to build faster Power Automate cloud flows, Power Apps, or Power Virtual Agents bots.

Virtual tables will also trigger the code on your F&O's data entities, so if you're initializing a field's value using the `initValue` method, creating a record using a virtual table will also do it.

> **Remember the licenses!**
>
> Although I mentioned this earlier, I would like to reiterate that you'll need an F&O license if you're an interactive user accessing the data in F&O when using virtual tables. The user also needs to exist in F&O. It's something you need to evaluate because depending on the business case you want to solve, you might want to use Dual-write instead.

Some use cases for virtual tables are as follows:

- **Seamless integration**: Virtual tables are ideal when you need seamless integration between Dynamics 365 F&O and Dataverse without data synchronization. They provide real-time access to F&O data, enabling you to build more efficient Power Automate cloud flows, Power Apps, or Power Virtual Agents bots.

- **CRUD operations**: Virtual tables support CRUD operations, making them a versatile tool for working with F&O data in Dataverse.

- **Calling F&O business logic in Dataverse**: Virtual tables allow you to execute F&O's data entity code and validations.

- **Reducing development effort**: By using virtual tables, you can build custom applications, workflows, and chatbots that interact with F&O data more easily and with less development effort.

- **Trigger data entities actions**: You can execute processes such as posting an invoice thanks to OData actions being available in Dataverse via virtual tables.

In conclusion, virtual tables offer a powerful and flexible solution for integrating Dynamics 365 F&O data with Dataverse. They provide real-time access, support CRUD operations, and allow for the execution of F&O's code. Virtual tables can help you build more efficient and consistent solutions across your organization's technology ecosystem.

Summary

In this chapter, we learned about Dual-write and virtual tables and how to create the link between a finance and operations environment and a Dataverse environment. This is achieved through the Power Platform integration, which has become a more streamlined process due to Microsoft's investments in the Convergence plan.

We also learned about Dual-write, which is an integration feature that synchronizes data between Dynamics 365 Finance and Operations and Dataverse. It ensures data consistency across your Dynamics 365 products, helping reduce errors and making processes more efficient.

Finally, we learned about virtual tables, formerly known as virtual entities, which allow for integration between Dynamics 365 F&O and Dataverse by displaying data from F&O within Dataverse without actually storing it there. This feature facilitates performing CRUD operations on the external data and makes it possible to use virtual tables as data sources in Power Automate, Power Apps, or Power Virtual Agents.

In the next chapter, we'll learn about process automation with Power Automate cloud flows, the different components (such as triggers or actions), and the connectors available when we want to connect to Dynamics 365 Finance and Operations Apps.

Questions

Here are some questions to test your understanding of the chapter. The answers to the questions are given at the end.

1. What is the primary purpose of Dual-write?

    a.   Synchronizing data between Dataverse and F&O in real-time

    b.   Storing data from F&O in Dataverse

    c.   Integrating data from multiple sources into Dataverse

    d.   Visualize data from F&O in Power Apps

2. What is the main advantage of virtual tables over Dual-write?

    a.   Faster synchronization between F&O and Dataverse

    b.   Storing data from F&O in Dataverse

    c.   Displaying data from F&O in Dataverse without storing it

    d.   Integrating data from multiple sources into F&O

3. What operations can be performed using virtual tables?

    a.   Only reading data

    b.   Only writing data

    c.   CRUD operations

    d.   None of the above

4. In which directions can Dual-write synchronize data?

    a.   From Dataverse to F&O

    b.   From F&O to Dataverse

    c.   Bidirectional

    d.   All of the above

5. When should you choose virtual tables over Dual-write?

   a. When you need to synchronize data between F&O and Dataverse

   b. When you don't need to synchronize data between F&O and Dataverse

   c. When you need to store data from F&O in Dataverse

   d. When you need to integrate data from multiple sources into F&O

Further reading

You can visit the following links if you want to learn more about the F&O and Power Platform integration:

Enable the Power Platform integration:

```
https://learn.microsoft.com/en-us/dynamics365/fin-ops-core/
dev-itpro/power-platform/enable-power-platform-integration
```

Dual-write:

```
https://learn.microsoft.com/en-us/dynamics365/fin-ops-core/
dev-itpro/data-entities/dual-write/dual-write-home-page
```

Dual-write solutions:

```
https://learn.microsoft.com/en-us/dynamics365/fin-ops-core/
dev-itpro/data-entities/dual-write/separated-solutions
```

Virtual tables:

```
https://learn.microsoft.com/en-us/dynamics365/fin-ops-core/
dev-itpro/power-platform/virtual-entities-overview
```

Answers

1. a. Synchronizing data between Dataverse and F&O in real-time

2. c. Displaying data from F&O in Dataverse without storing it

3. c. CRUD operations

4. d. All of the above

5. b. When you don't need to synchronize data between F&O and Dataverse

Part 2: Extending Dynamics 365 F&O with Power Platform

In this part, we'll explore the use of Power Automate and Power Apps to enhance the capabilities of Dynamics 365 Finance and Operations Apps. We will also cover the process of exporting F&O data to use it in Power BI and other BI tools with the aid of Azure Data Lake and Synapse link.

This part has the following chapters:

- *Chapter 3, Power Automate Flows in Dynamics 365*
- *Chapter 4, Replacing F&O Processes with Power Automate*
- *Chapter 5, Building Automations and Integrations*
- *Chapter 6, Power Apps: What's in It for Finance and Operations Consultants?*
- *Chapter 7, Extend F&O Apps with Power Apps*
- *Chapter 8, Power BI Reporting for Dynamics 365 F&O Apps*

3

Power Automate Flows in Dynamics 365

With Power Automate cloud flows, we will be able to automate processes in Dynamics 365 Finance and Operations Apps thanks to low-code. This will also create integrations with third parties thanks to its large collection of connectors without having to develop X++ code. The goal of this chapter is to learn about Power Automate, the different types of cloud flows and connectors, and how we can use them with Dynamics 365 F&O to speed up development.

To follow along some of the sections of this chapter, you'll need access to a Power Platform environment. We will explore the following in this chapter:

- What is Power Automate, and why should I use another tool for my processes?
- Scheduled, instant, and automated cloud flows
- Power Automate connectors
- Dynamics 365 Finance and Operations standard connectors or Dataverse connectors?

What is Power Automate, and why should I use another tool for my processes?

Power Automate is the Power Platform component that's used to automate business processes, in a low-code manner – in the cloud or in a PC. It is extremely useful when it comes to taking over tasks that are time-consuming or repetitive.

> **Logic Apps' smaller brother**
>
> If you've worked with Azure integration services, you might already know about Logic Apps. We could say that Power Automate is its "little brother." Logic Apps is targeted toward IT professionals and Power Automate to end users, but in the end, both products do more or less the same. In this chapter, we will be focusing on cloud flows. However, it's also possible to run Power Automate flows on your PC with Desktop flows, add **robotic process automation** (**RPA**) to your desktop computer, and automate repetitive processes that will later run unattended.

If you think of automated and unattended processes running in Dynamics 365 Finance and Operations, the first thing that will come to your mind will be batch jobs. So, you can think of Power Automate cloud flows as something that can do some of the things a batch job would do, but that's not all; it can do more than just run processes on a schedule.

Aren't batch jobs and X++ enough?

You might be thinking: why should we be using a different tool, or another tool when we can do almost everything we need inside the ERP? You may also wonder whether adding an extra layer to your solution is worth the effort.

What if I told you that this additional layer, which is Power Automate, could help you change processes faster than if you did it using X++? How can that be?

It's easy; think about what you need to do when you want to change X++ code and update production: change the code, release the code to a sandbox environment, do some testing, and then schedule the production update. We're talking about the range of hours to do all of this and depending on your company's processes to allow a production update, it could be days. Now, consider this scenario: you've implemented a Power Automate cloud flow that manages some F&O processes. Even in this case, if your organization has an approval process to release changes to production, you'd still need to go through it. However, by using Power Automate, you can save time because you just have to change the flow and there is no release to sandbox or production. This will help to make the process more streamlined and efficient.

> **Decoupling**
>
> So, while it may seem that incorporating Power Automate into your solution might increase dependencies, it actually enhances decoupling. By acting as an intermediate layer that can quickly and flexibly respond to changes, Power Automate reduces the reliance of your processes on X++ code modifications.

This results in a more adaptable solution that can quickly adjust to meet your business needs, effectively demonstrating the decoupling benefits of Power Automate. So, adding Power Automate as an extra layer to your solution is not merely worth the effort but also a strategic move to increase efficiency and adaptability. Hence our answer to whether or not Power Automate can help us quicken our processes is an emphatic "yes."

Now that we know a bit about Power Automate, let's learn about the different cloud flows that we can use.

Scheduled, instant, and automated cloud flows

When you create a Power Automate cloud flow, you can choose among three different cloud flow types (see *Figure 3.1*):

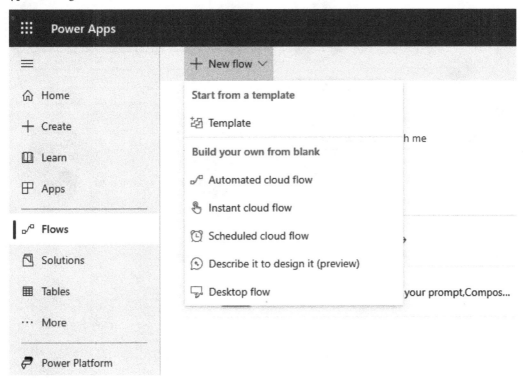

Figure 3.1 – Power Automate cloud flow types

In the maker portal, when you click **New flow**, you can choose between **Automated**, **Instant**, or **Scheduled** cloud flows. The difference between these three types is the trigger they use, which is the starting step of a flow – the action that will start the process:

- Automated cloud flows are triggered by events
- Instant cloud flows are started by clicking a button
- Scheduled cloud flows run on a schedule

In the next sections, we will learn more details about each of these flow types, how they're triggered, and the differences that exist between them.

Automated cloud flows

Automated cloud flow triggers are event-based; for example, an F&O business event, receiving an email, or having a new file created in **OneDrive** (see *Figure 3.2*):

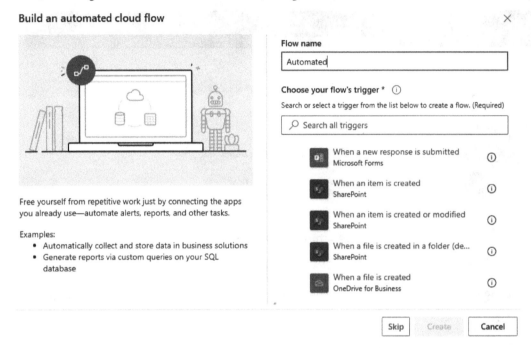

Figure 3.2 – Automated cloud flows creation dialog

When you select an automated cloud flow, you get some triggers in the wizard dialog. If you want to search for the F&O trigger, you need to search for f in & ops. This should lead you to the **Business Events** trigger (see *Figure 3.3*):

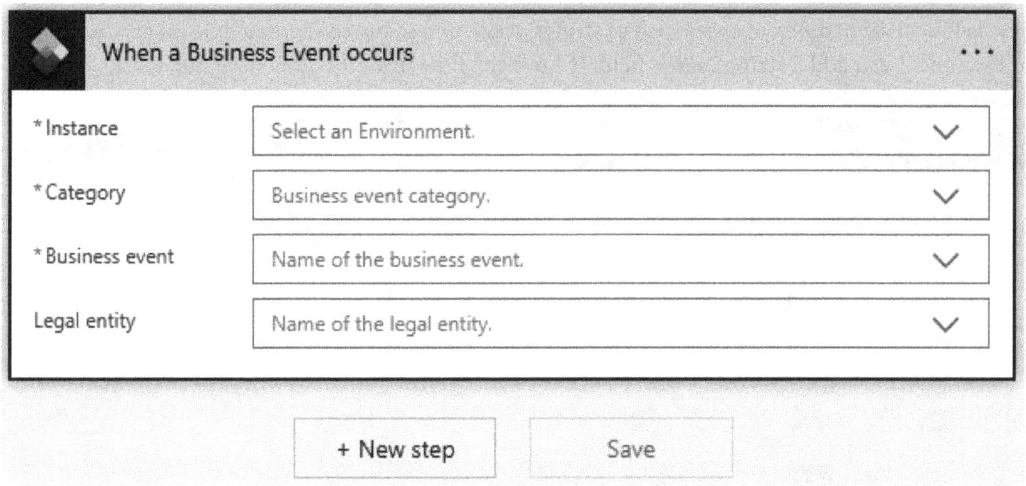

Figure 3.3 – Business Events trigger

This is the only native F&O trigger you'll find, and by completing the three mandatory **Instance**, **Category**, and **Business event** fields, you will be able to start a flow when that business event's conditions are met in F&O.

> **Note**
>
> You don't need to configure the business event on the F&O side when you want to use it; just add it to your flow as a trigger, and that will activate it in the instance that you select.

Instant cloud flows

Instant cloud flows can be used directly from your mobile device via the Power Automate app, giving you the flexibility to trigger processes on the go. In an instant flow, you can add input fields that will need to be filled in before triggering an action (see *Figure 3.4*):

Figure 3.4 – Instant cloud flow trigger

These fields can be of different types such as strings, dates, and so on, so there's a little bit of validation. For example, I can add a string **Name** field. If I test the flow from the flow designer, it asks for the field (see *Figure 3.5*):

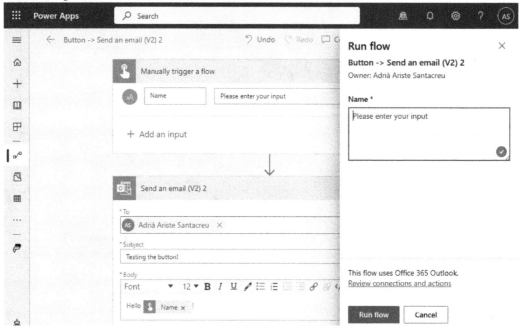

Figure 3.5 – Instant flow with input fields

When testing it, or using the mobile app, the **Name** field that I added becomes mandatory. And then, you can use it in the following flow steps.

Scheduled cloud flows

These are the ones that remind us the most about F&O's batch jobs. Scheduled cloud flows run on a schedule, where you can select a recurrence and make the flow run on an hourly, daily, weekly, and so on basis (see *Figure 3.6*):

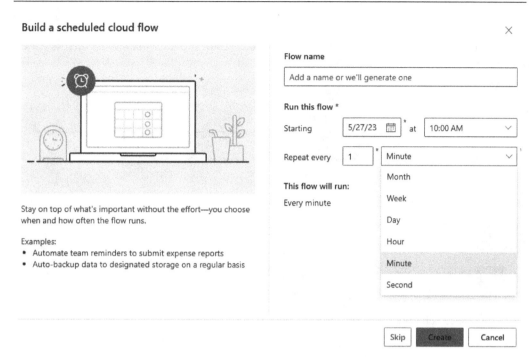

Build a scheduled cloud flow

Stay on top of what's important without the effort—you choose when and how often the flow runs.

Examples:
- Automate team reminders to submit expense reports
- Auto-backup data to designated storage on a regular basis

Flow name

Add a name or we'll generate one

Run this flow *

Starting   5/27/23   at   10:00 AM

Repeat every   1   Minute

This flow will run:

Every minute

Month

Week

Day

Hour

Minute

Second

Skip   Create   Cancel

Figure 3.6 – Scheduled flow creation wizard

In the creation wizard, you can define the recurrence the flow must have. We can even make it run every second! Just select a starting date and time, and the flow will start repeating the actions after your desired setup.

Now, we're going to learn about connectors, the blocks that we will use to execute actions after they are triggered.

Power Automate connectors

We've learned about one of the key components of Power Automate: *triggers*. Triggers are the actions that start a flow. Now, we're going to learn about connectors, which are the "boxes" that will let us connect to services and use them in our Power Automate flows.

We can think of these connectors, displayed as boxes in the UI, as wrappers around each of the services' APIs that allow users to easily access the APIs in a low-code manner. These boxes are the bridges between the Power Automate platform and other services, regardless of whether they are Microsoft services or third-party services. At the moment of writing this book, there are over 1,000 connectors available, which allow the creation of integrations with a diverse set of services. These services go from Microsoft productivity tools such as Microsoft 365, SharePoint, or Teams to other services such as Salesforce, Google services, and many more.

Every connector may have a different set of available actions, depending on the features and functions of the service behind it. For example, the SharePoint connector provides operations such as **Add attachment**, **Create file**, or **Update item** (see *Figure 3.7*):

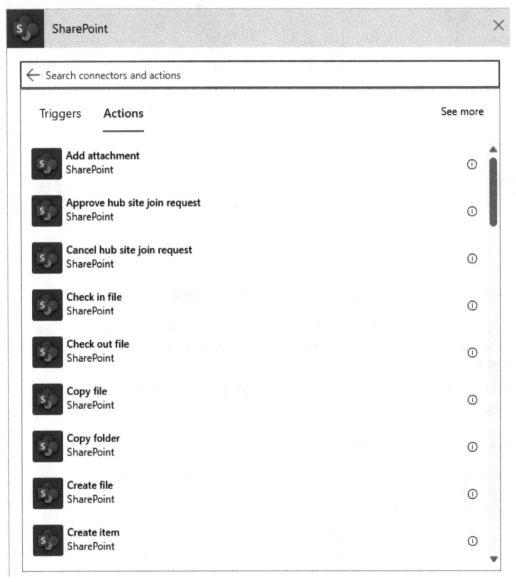

Figure 3.7 – Power Automate connector actions

When you select a connector, you will see a list of possible triggers that it has if you're selecting the first step of your flow, and actions if you're selecting the next steps.

Connector types

There are different connector categories depending on their characteristics:

- **Standard connectors**: Out-of-the-box connectors that can be used in all Power Automate plans; for example, the ones you can access with your Microsoft 365 license. See a full list here: `https://learn.microsoft.com/en-us/connectors/connector-reference/connector-reference-standard-connectors`.

- **Premium connectors**: Connectors that require you to have a Power Automate plan license. For example, the Dynamics 365 F&O connector falls under this category. These are all the premium connectors: `https://learn.microsoft.com/en-us/connectors/connector-reference/connector-reference-premium-connectors`.

- **Custom connectors**: These are the connectors built by you and are available in your tenant.

Power Automate is a cloud service, but it can access your on-premises data thanks to the on-premises data gateway: once you've installed it, you can access some services in Power Automate using your data.

Note

Access to different connector levels depends on your Power Automate license. Depending on which connectors you need to use, you will have to purchase different licenses.

The connector framework is one of the key features of Power Automate, enabling users to interact seamlessly with multiple services from one central platform and streamline their workflows.

Dynamics 365 Finance and Operations standard connectors or Dataverse connectors?

Now that we've learned a bit about connectors, I'll try to answer the question that heads this section so that you can choose which one is best depending on your requirements.

Connectors

We will be comparing the Fin & Ops Apps (Dynamics 365) connector and the Microsoft Dataverse connector (see *Figure 3.8*):

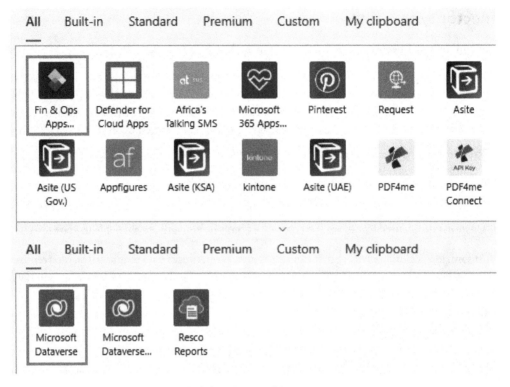

Figure 3.8 – Fin & Ops Apps and Dataverse connectors

If you look for fin & ops and dataverse, you will be able to select the connectors. Also, beware because there's still the legacy Dataverse connector available. The one you need to use is the green one; the gray one is suffixed with the legacy text and you must avoid using it.

Triggers

For the Finance and Operations connector, we only have one possible trigger, the one for business events that we saw previously when we learned about automated cloud flows.

If you go to the **Business events** catalog in F&O and exclude the workflow-related business events, you will see just over 30 available business events. That's not a lot. It's actually very limited considering the number of tables that exist in the system, and could potentially trigger a business event on all CRUD operations, right?

Fortunately, we also have data events! Data events are events based on CRUD operations done to public data entities, which are the ones that can throw a data event. In contrast to business events, which can only send a limited amount of data, data events send the complete entity record in the payload. However, there is a single limitation in this case. Virtual fields and computed columns in data entities, for instance, won't be able to trigger a data event.

If we go to the **Business events** form and select the **Data event catalog** tab, you'll see many more records than in the **Business events** catalog – actually, over 9,000 operations for data entities. If you filter on the **Customers V3** entity, you'll see three records (see *Figure 3.9*):

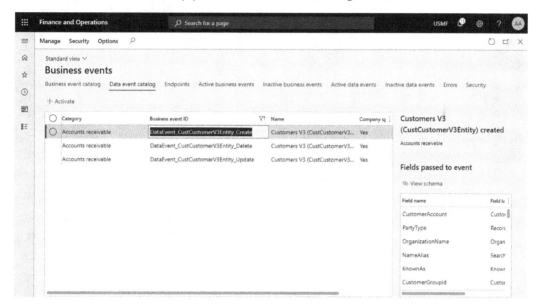

Figure 3.9 – Business events catalog for Customers V3 entity

These three records appear for create, delete, or update operations, and you can enable the operations separately.

> **A little trick**
>
> When we activate any of the operations, it will turn on the virtual table feature for the Dataverse entity linked to that operation – as long as the virtual table hasn't already been turned on. And you can forget about the **Advanced find** form in the old **CRM settings** menu we saw in the previous chapter.

And how is this related to triggers?

Well, once we enable data events, we can use them as a Dataverse trigger! If we create a new automated cloud flow and select the Dataverse connector, we'll see three of them (see *Figure 3.10*):

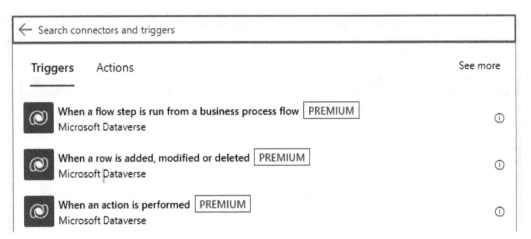

Figure 3.10 – Dataverse triggers

The trigger that we'll be using is the one named **When a row is added, modified or deleted**, which will make use of the data events. Select the trigger, and in the **Table name** field, look for **mserp** (see *Figure 3.11*):

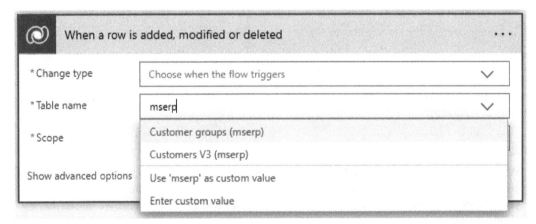

Figure 3.11 – F&O-activated entities

This will display all F&O data entities whose Virtual tables are enabled on Dataverse. In the **Change type** field, you can select different values depending on what you want to trigger the flow on:

- Added

- Added or Deleted

- Added or Modified

- Added or Modified or Deleted
- Deleted
- Modified
- Modified or Deleted

In the **Scope** field, you have to select **Organization**, which will be the company from which the data event is triggered.

Data events and legal entities

When you enable a data event, you select in which legal entity it becomes active. If you want to enable it in multiple legal entities, you'll have to activate it for each one of them. For data entities that have no company context, their business events will be enabled system-wide.

And now, knowing these things about the F&O and Dataverse connectors, which one would you use? It's easy for me: the Dataverse connector with F&O data events.

Why? As we've seen, we only have around 30 business events out of the box, and we'd have to create new ones using X++ if we wanted to add new trigger points in the code. If we go with the data catalog and its data events, we can use all existing public data entities as triggers.

For example, no business event triggers when a customer is created, so if we wanted to use a business event for that, we would have to create all the business event classes and extend CustTable's insert method. Instead, we can just enable the data event for the **Customers V3** data entity and use it as a trigger with the Dataverse connector. And to me, that makes data events a clear choice!

Actions

Now it's time for a fight between the Finance and Operations and Dataverse connectors' actions. I'll show how we can update a customer group record using the F&O connector and the Dataverse connector. In both scenarios, we will use the Dataverse trigger we've just learned about. Let's start with the Dataverse one! The trigger is a new customer being created in Finance and Operations. Thus, using the customer group of the customer, we'll update some customer group information (see Figure 3.12):

Figure 3.12 – Flow using Dataverse connector's action to update a record

When a customer is created, we get all the customer data as the output of the trigger; we can use that later. As the second step, we need to retrieve the rows from Dataverse before being able to update the record, using the **Filter rows** field on the **List rows** action.

Why is that? Can't we update the record without that extra step?

The answer is no, and the reason is that the **Update a row** action for Dataverse expects the **Row ID** field to identify the record on Dataverse, and we don't have that on the payload of the data event.

Now, let's take a look at how we do it with the F&O connector. The scenario is the same. We trigger the flow using the Dataverse trigger on the **Customers V3** Virtual table and want to update something for customer groups (see *Figure 3.13*):

(⊘) When a row is added, modified or deleted		···
* Change type	Added or Modified or Deleted	∨
* Table name	Customers V3 (mserp)	∨
* Scope	Organization	∨
Show advanced options ∨		

◆ Update a record		···
* Instance		∨
* Entity name	CustomerGroups	∨
* Object id	[⊘] Company Code × , [⊘] Customer group ×	
* Customer group	[⊘] Customer group ×	
Company	[⊘] Company Code ×	
Show advanced options ∨		

Figure 3.13 – Automated flow using F&O update action

In this flow, we don't need the intermediate step to retrieve a record, because the F&O **Update a record** action is using the fields we already have to update the customer group, which are the fields that the natural key of the data entity has. For customer groups, that's the `DataAreaId` and `CustomerGroupId` values.

We could say the winner here is the Finance and Operations connector. However, in my opinion, it's not such a clear win as with the triggers.

To summarize, it's a good idea to use the Dataverse trigger because it saves us from having to create new business events using the F&O trigger. And for the actions, it will depend on what you want to do!

Summary

Power Automate lets users automate business processes with a low-code approach. It can run tasks in the cloud or on a PC, targeting repetitive or time-consuming tasks and thereby freeing users from performing them manually. This automation can be executed through cloud flows, which are similar to batch jobs in Dynamics 365 Finance and Operations, but with the added versatility of not just running processes on a schedule.

In addition to standardizing and automating workflows, Power Automate can enhance integrations with third-party services. It achieves this through an extensive collection of connectors, sparing us from developing X++ code. This functionality allows for more efficient changes to processes, reducing the time required for updating the code, releasing it to a sandbox environment, testing, and scheduling the production update. Thus, Power Automate acts as a rapid and adaptable intermediate layer, reducing the reliance of your processes on X++ code modifications and enhancing decoupling.

Power Automate cloud flows can be scheduled, instant, or automated. Scheduled flows run on a set schedule, instant flows are initiated by user actions, and automated flows are triggered by events.

The choice between Dynamics 365 Finance and Operations standard connectors and Dataverse connectors will depend on your specific needs. Each connector has unique features, with Dataverse offering a more extensive selection of business events. As for actions, it again depends on the specific use case, with both connectors offering different advantages. Therefore, Power Automate, with its ability to automate tasks, integrate with third-party services, and offer flexibility in triggers and actions, provides a robust tool for enhancing business processes.

In the next chapter, we'll learn how we can use Power Automate flows to process Dynamics 365 F&O workflows and send notifications to assigned users in Teams.

Questions

Here are some questions to test your understanding of the chapter. The answers to the questions are given at the end.

1. What is Power Automate primarily used for?

   a. Automating email responses

   b. Creating graphic design elements

   c. Developing X++ code

   d. Automating business processes in a low-code manner

2. Which of the following is *NOT* a type of cloud flow in Power Automate?

   a. Automated cloud flow

   b. Instant cloud flow

   c.   Scheduled cloud flow

   d.   Periodic cloud flow

3.   Which of the following is an advantage of using Power Automate as an additional layer in your solution?

   a.   It enhances decoupling and allows quicker changes in processes.

   b.   It improves your ability to develop X++ code.

   c.   It eliminates the need for third-party connectors.

   d.   It completely replaces the need for batch jobs in Dynamics 365 Finance and Operations.

4.   What are connectors in the context of Power Automate?

   a.   They are scripts that need to be coded in X++.

   b.   They are the components that enable Power Automate to connect with other services.

   c.   They are hardware components that establish physical connections between servers.

   d.   They are a type of cloud flow, similar to automated or instant flows.

5.   Between the Finance and Operations connector and the Microsoft Dataverse connector, which one is favored for triggering due to the number of available events?

   a.   The Finance and Operations connector because it provides a large number of business events.

   b.   The Microsoft Dataverse connector because it makes use of data events and provides a wider range of trigger points.

   c.   Both are equally favored because they offer the same number of events.

   d.   Neither, as both require X++ coding to create new trigger points.

Further reading

To know more about Power Automate flows you can visit the following links.

Power Automate documentation: `https://learn.microsoft.com/en-us/power-automate/`

Power Automate vs Logic Apps: `https://learn.microsoft.com/en-us/microsoft-365/community/power-automate-vs-logic-apps`

Automated cloud flows: `https://learn.microsoft.com/en-us/power-automate/get-started-logic-flow`

Scheduled cloud flows: `https://learn.microsoft.com/en-us/power-automate/run-scheduled-tasks`

Instant flows: `https://learn.microsoft.com/en-us/power-automate/introduction-to-button-flows`

Power Automate connectors: `https://learn.microsoft.com/en-us/connectors/connector-reference/connector-reference-powerautomate-connectors`

On-premises data gateway: `https://learn.microsoft.com/en-us/power-automate/gateway-reference`

Fin & Ops Apps connector: `https://learn.microsoft.com/en-us/connectors/dynamicsax/`

Microsoft Dataverse connector: `https://learn.microsoft.com/en-us/connectors/commondataserviceforapps/`

Data events: `https://learn.microsoft.com/en-us/dynamics365/fin-ops-core/dev-itpro/business-events/data-events`

Answers

1. d. Automating business processes in a low-code manner

2. d. Periodic cloud flow

3. a. It enhances decoupling and allows quicker changes in processes.

4. b. They are the components that enable Power Automate to connect with other services.

5. b. The Microsoft Dataverse connector because it makes use of data events and provides a wider range of trigger points.

4

Replacing F&O Processes with Power Automate

In this chapter, we will learn how to extend the standard F&O workflow functionality into Microsoft Teams with Power Automate. We will learn about OData actions in Power Automate, how we can complete the approval process of an existing workflow, and how users can approve or reject them from Teams or via emails.

The scenario demonstrated in this chapter will be creating a purchase requisition and submitting the workflow in F&O. After this, Power Automate will process the approval in Teams or through an email. The purchase requisition will have the workflow enabled at the header level only.

In this chapter, we will cover the following:

- F&O Business events, our workflow trigger
- Using OData actions
- Making messages user-friendly
- Processing the workflow elements
- Managing the approval process on Teams
- Approvals using email

Technical requirements

If you followed the setup steps in *Chapter 2*, you should have all the technical requirements.

Additionally, the data used will be from the demo Contoso database.

The code needed for some of the steps of this chapter can be found on GitHub at `https://github.com/PacktPublishing/Extending-D365-Finance-and-Operation-apps-with-Power-Platform-/tree/main/Chapter%2004`.

F&O Business events, our workflow trigger

In the previous chapter, we learned about the Power Automate triggers that we can use for F&O, business events, and data events. Based on a small comparison, we concluded that using data events is the best decision.

Now forget about that! That conclusion was based on insert, update, or delete operations at the table level, but for this chapter, we're going to use the workflow business events because they're available out of the box in the catalog and cover all the needs to solve the scenario of approving Dynamics 365 F&O workflows in Teams or email.

Workflow business events

The business event we'll be using is the one called **Purchase requisition review (000062) - Approve purchase requisitions** in the category **Workflow workitem** (see *Figure 4.1*):

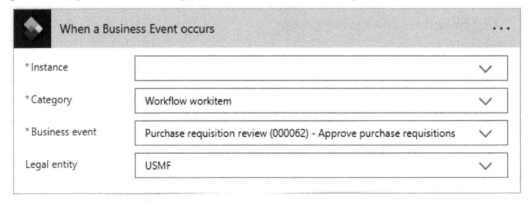

Figure 4.1 – Purchase requisition workflow trigger

Select the instance where the workflow will be triggered first, and then, in the **Category** field, select **Workflow workitem**. This will filter the available elements in the **Business event** field. Then, we must select **Purchase requisition review (000062) - Approve purchase requisitions**.

Now we're ready to recover the content returned by the trigger and parse it.

> **Parse... what?**
>
> You might not know what parsing is, and we're going to use it quite a lot. Parsing in the context of JSON involves interpreting the JSON formatted data, transforming the text-based information into a data structure that can be easily manipulated by a program.
>
> This process allows us to get meaningful information from the JSON file, such as arrays, objects, and values, making it possible to use the data in various applications in an easier manner.

Parse the response

The output of the trigger is a JSON text that corresponds to the payload of the **Business event**, which we can get from the business events workspace (see *Figure 4.2*):

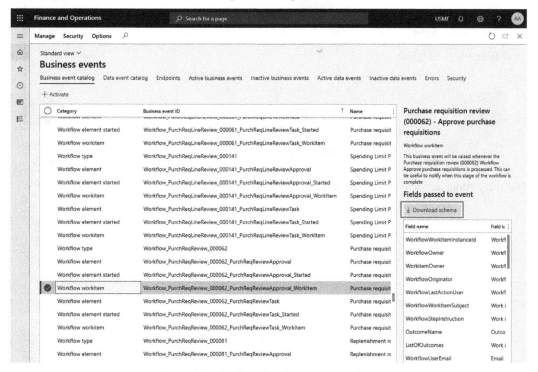

Figure 4.2 – Getting a business event payload

In the workspace, select the business event with the JSON you want to know about and click the **Download schema** link on the right. A file will be downloaded with sample data.

Why do we need this? Isn't the output of the trigger step enough? It is, but it's not very user-friendly. That's why we'll use the Parse JSON action (see *Figure 4.3*):

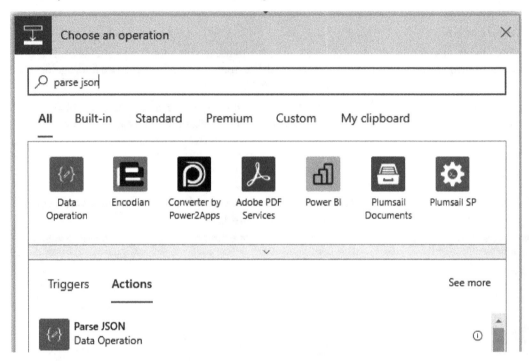

Figure 4.3 – The Parse JSON action

Select this action, and in its **Content** field, select the body of the previous step (see *Figure 4.4*):

Figure 4.4 – Parse JSON with schema

Now we need to fill in the **Schema** field that tells the **Parse JSON** action which elements exist in the JSON output from the business event. The Parse JSON action will take that JSON content and then make each element in the JSON file available as a single identifiable field in the Power Automate editor. This will make it more user-friendly to select the value of the members later.

To do this, click the **Generate from sample** button and paste the content of the file we downloaded earlier. Click the **Done** button to fill in the **Schema** field automatically.

We can access the members of the JSON file easily. The next step will be using them to validate whether we can process the workflow message with OData actions.

> **What is OData?**
>
> **OData**, which is short for **Open Data Protocol**, is a web protocol that allows for the querying and updating of data over the internet using REST APIs in a simple and standard way. OData aims to simplify data sharing across disparate systems and applications through a standardized protocol.

Using OData actions

In the next step, we'll call an OData action to validate whether the workflow step can be completed. OData actions are special methods executed on data entities that are decorated with the `SysODataAction` attribute. For example, the validate method looks as follows:

```
[SysODataAction('validate', false), Hookable(false)]
public static boolean validate(WorkflowWorkItemInstanceId
WorkflowWorkItemInstanceId)
```

We can see that the method takes one parameter. When calling the action from Postman, for example, we need to include the parameters in the JSON body of the request. To do it in Power Automate, we can use the **Execute action** action of the F&O connector (see *Figure 4.5*):

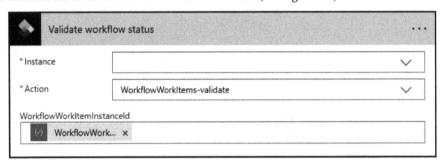

Figure 4.5 – Using the execute action

When you select the OData action, the Power Automate action will update its UI and you will see a new field for each parameter that the action you've selected has. In the case of the validate action, it's asking for the **WorkflowWorkItemInstanceId** parameter due to the **Parse JSON** step we did previously. We'll see all the elements of the JSON file as individual fields (see *Figure 4.6*):

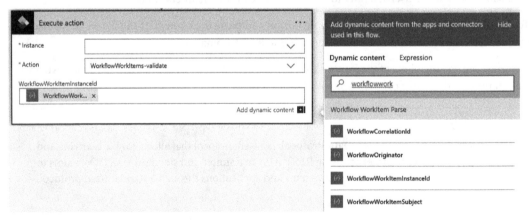

Figure 4.6 – Selectable dynamic content

For our action, we must select the **WorkflowWorkItemInstanceId** field from the previous step. In this case, it has the same name as the parameter.

Validate the workflow

Once this action runs, we will add a **Condition** action to check if the return value is true. If it is true, then we will continue with the remaining steps; otherwise, we'll take no further action.

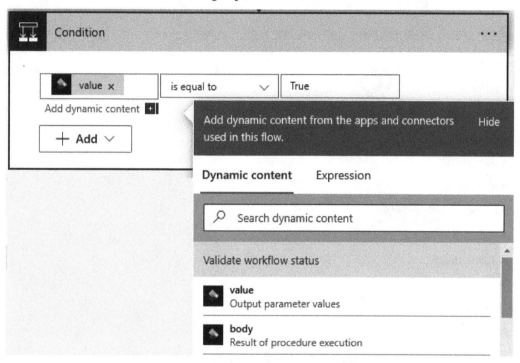

Figure 4.7 – Evaluating the output of the WF validate action

We will take the value output and the comparison is equal to True. Don't forget the capital T; the evaluation is case-sensitive.

Once we know we can process the workflow message, we need to send the user a message to take action. With the help of adaptive cards, we can make the messages in Teams user friendly. Once the workflow message has been validated, we continue working on the **If yes** branch and start building what the user will see on Teams. To do this, we will use Adaptive Cards. **Adaptive cards** are an open standard format that allow developers to create UI components uniformly by using JSON to define its structure. Let's take a look at them.

Creating an adaptive card

Designing an adaptive card is really easy with its designer, which you can access at `https://adaptivecards.io/designer`. There, we will select the Microsoft Teams host app and create a new blank card (see *Figure 4.8*):

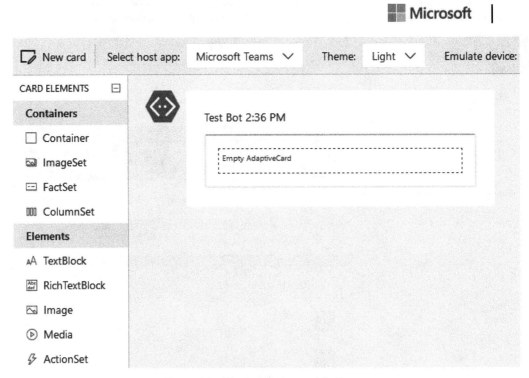

Figure 4.8 – Blank adaptive card for Teams

On the left side, we have the drag-and-drop elements we can add to the card. We will choose a **TextBlock** and an **ActionSet** element (see *Figure 4.9*):

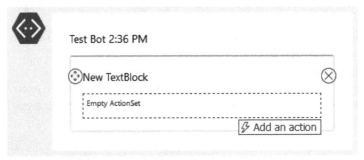

Figure 4.9 – ActionSet element

When you hover with the mouse on the **ActionSet** element, you will see the **Add an action** button. We need to add three buttons: **Approve** and **Reject** of type **Submit** and a **View** button of type **OpenUrl**. Select the first button on the **CARD STRUCTURE** pane to set some properties (see *Figure 4.10*):

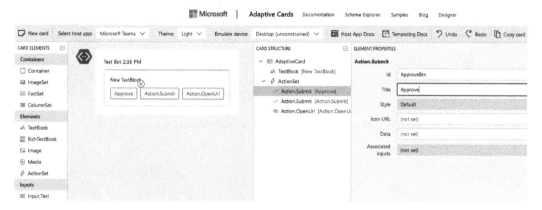

Figure 4.10 – Property Editor on adaptive cards

Like in Visual Studio, we can edit the properties of the elements on the right pane. We will change the **Id** of the Approve button to ApproveBtn and its title to Approve. Next, select the second button, which will be Reject, and change the **Id** to RejectBtn and **Title** to Reject. Finally, select the last button. Change its **Id** to ViewBtn and its and **Title** to View. Add something to the **URL** field as a placeholder. We'll take care of that later.

Posting an adaptive card to Teams

Now, on the bottom pane of the web page, you'll see the **Card Payload Editor** box. We will use its content in a minute. Now we go back to the Power Automate designer, and in the **If yes** branch, add a new **Compose** action that we'll call Adaptive card body (see *Figure 4.11*):

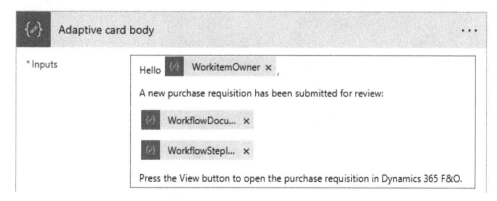

Figure 4.11 – Adaptive card text

Here, we will create the text we want to add to the adaptive card in the `TextBlock` element we created in the previous step. You can customize this text to your needs. I have added the name of the current assignee, some text, and the `WorkflowDocument` and `WorkflowStepInstruction` texts.

Create another **Compose** action and paste the JSON content of the **Card Payload Editor** box (see *Figure 4.12*):

Figure 4.12 – Adaptive card JSON with our values

Remove the text member content of the `TextBlock` and use the output of the text we've created in the previous **Compose** action. In the **Url** field, delete the placeholder we created earlier and select the **LinkToWeb** field of the trigger's output.

We have our adaptive card customized and now it's time to use it. Add a new action of the type **Post adaptive card** and wait for a response (see *Figure 4.13*):

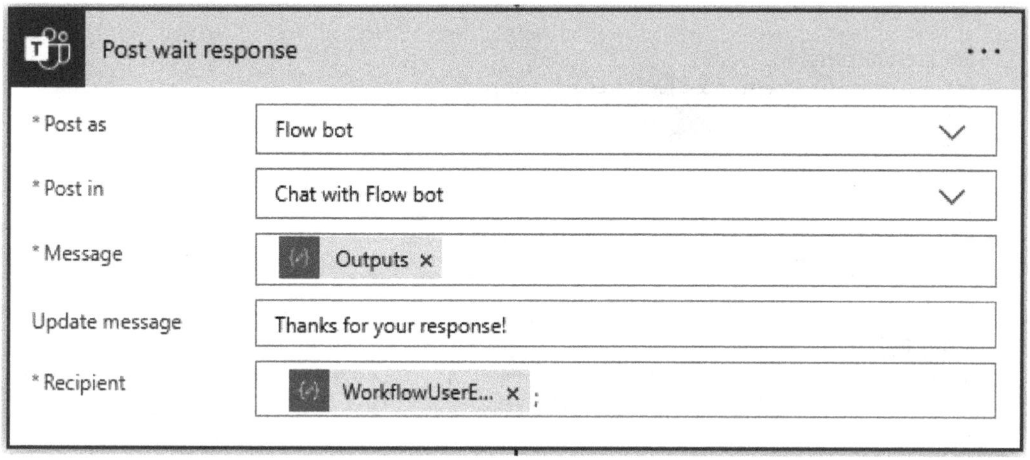

Post wait response		...

* Post as	Flow bot	∨
* Post in	Chat with Flow bot	∨
* Message	Outputs ×	
Update message	Thanks for your response!	
* Recipient	WorkflowUserE... ×	

Figure 4.13 – The Post adaptive card action and waiting for a response

This action allows us to post a message via a flow bot to a Teams channel, chat, or group chat. In our case, we'll select the chat option. In the **Message** field, select the output of the previous **Compose** action, the one with our customized JSON, and in the **Recipient** field, select the `WorkflowUserEmail` field from the trigger. This is the email of the user that has this workflow step assigned.

This action will send a Teams message to the user and keep the flow running until we get an answer. Flow can wait up to 30 days for a response, though this can be configured. We can agree that 30 days is too much time for approval workflows and to keep the flow running. We will set a timeout of 15 minutes for this step, but you can define something else depending on your needs. Click on the three dots next to the action name and choose the **Settings** option. After clicking it, the box will show the settings for that action (see *Figure 4.14*):

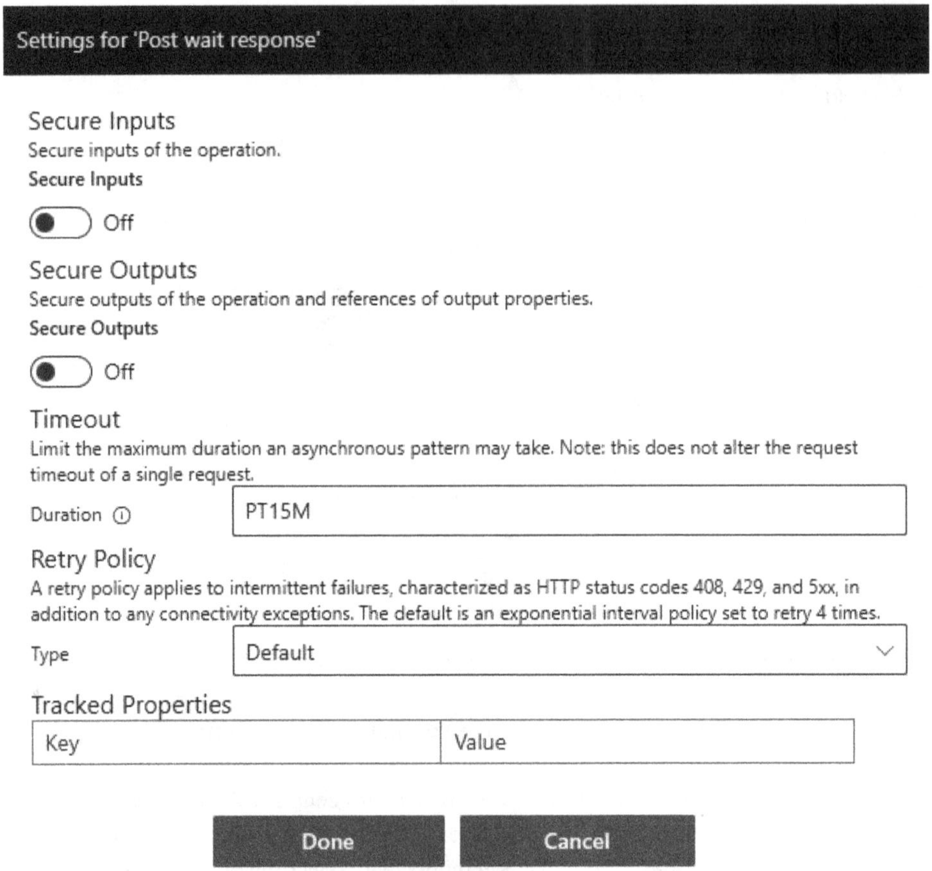

Figure 4.14 – Defining the timeout in the action settings

In the **Timeout** section, set the **Duration** to PT15M. What does PT15M mean? The Duration field uses the ISO8601 format. PT implies that it's time-related information, and 15M means 15 minutes. For example, PT1H1M1S would be the time for one hour, one minute, and one second. Again, you can set the amount of time you need here; 15 minutes is just a good value for this exercise.

The next step will be getting the user's response and acting accordingly by either approving or rejecting the workflow.

Processing the workflow elements

Now we need to add a parallel branch as our next step. The reason we do this is because the previous step will have two different outcomes. You get the first outcome if the user takes an action and the second outcome if they don't and the card times out. Click the + button below the last action and select **Add a parallel branch** (see *Figure 4.15*):

Add an action

Add a parallel branch

Figure 4.15 – Parallel branch

Processing the response

A parallel branch allows us to run actions simultaneously, but we will use it to manage the timeout outcome of the **Post adaptive card** and wait for a response" action. First, we will finish the left side of our flow, the one that processes the response from Teams. Add a new **Compose** action where we will add the body of the response. Since this action was released in preview, its output hasn't been displayed on the **Dynamic content** pane. This is why we need to manage it ourselves.

What we will do first is go to the Post adaptive card and wait for a response action. Click on the three dots and change its name to something shorter and without spaces, such as Post_wait_response. The reason for doing this is to be able to use the name of the action in the next step. We will use this later, and sometimes spaces are problematic. In the **Compose Input** write this:

```
outputs('Post_wait_response')?['body']
```

Post_wait_response is the name you have given to your action. This will retrieve the body of the response.

Before continuing, we will make sure this branch will be run when the response is sent and there is no timeout. Click on the three dots of this **Compose** action and select **Configure run after**. When you do this, we will see different options that we can select (see *Figure 4.16*):

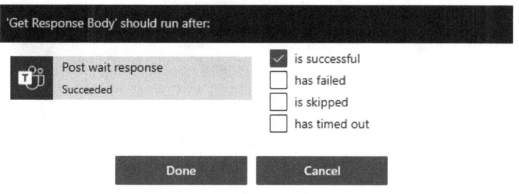

Figure 4.16 – Configuring run after options

By default, the **is successful** option is selected, and in this case, we don't need to change it.

Now add a **Parse JSON** action and set its content as the output of the **Compose** action we've just created. You can get the payload for the schema to run a test of the flow, but here, I leave the schema (not the payload) so you can use it:

```
{
    "type": "object",
    "properties": {
        "responseTime": {
            "type": "string"
        },
        "responder": {
            "type": "object",
            "properties": {
                "objectId": {
                    "type": "string"
                },
                "tenantId": {
                    "type": "string"
                },
                "email": {
                    "type": "string"
                },
                "userPrincipalName": {
                    "type": "string"
                },
                "displayName": {
                    "type": "string"
                }
            }
        },
        "submitActionId": {
            "type": "string"
        },
        "messageId": {
            "type": "string"
        },
        "messageLink": {
            "type": "string"
        }
    }
}
```

Now it's time to process the response, which can be an approval or a rejection. This means we need to add a **Condition** action and check how the user responded (see *Figure 4.17*):

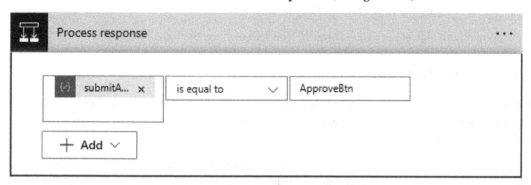

Figure 4.17 – Condition checking the outcome

In the condition, add the `submitActionId` field from the previous **Compose** action where we parsed the JSON from the response. Check if it is equal to `ApproveBtn`. This needs to be the same as the **Id** you defined for your `Approve` button when creating the adaptive card!

Finally, in the **If yes** and **If no** outcomes, we will approve or reject the workflow, respectively (see *Figure 4.18*):

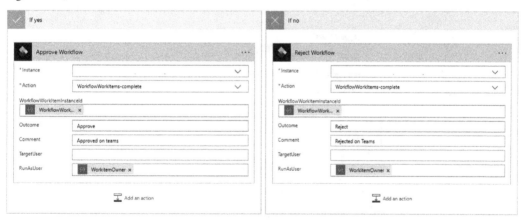

Figure 4.18 – Approval or rejection of the workflow

For each outcome, we will add an **Execute action** action from the F&O connector, and we will call the `WorflowWorkItem-complete` action in both cases. Use the same `WorkflowWorkItemInstanceId` fields as we did in the validate action for both too.

Now, for the Approve action, you need to set the **Outcome** field to `Approve`. You can add a comment if you want, which will appear on the workflow history in F&O. For the `Reject` action you must set the **Outcome** field to `Reject`.

For both actions, you need to set the `RunAsUser` field to the `WorkitemOwner` value. Otherwise, the workflow will fail the execution if the user under whom the flow runs is not the same as the one approving or rejecting the step, which will be the case.

We're done on this side of the parallel branch. Now let's work on the timeout.

Processing a timeout

We defined a 15-minute timeout for the **Post and wait for response** action. What do we do with it when there's a timeout? What I will do is inform the user that the message I sent them has expired and that they need to go into Dynamics 365 F&O to complete the workflow.

To do this, I've created an adaptive card where I inform the user that the previous message has timed out. The card has a button to go to the purchase requisition that needs to be approved (see *Figure 4.19*):

Figure 4.19 – Timeout adaptive card

The JSON for the adaptive card can be obtained from the designer page, as we saw before. This time, the text is informing the user that the previous card they got has timed out, and we point them to the Dynamics 365 F&O UI.

> **Note**
>
> When an action times out the actions of the buttons, approval or rejection won't be completed even if the buttons are pressed.

As we did before with the successful side of the parallel branch, we now need to click the three dots of this **Compose** action and select **Configure run after**. Select **has timed out** for this side (see *Figure 4.20*):

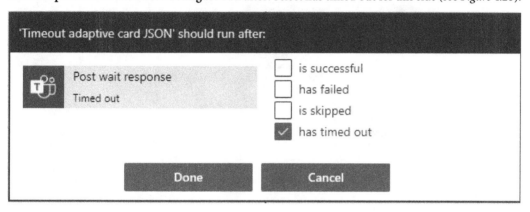

Figure 4.20 – Running the action when the previous one times out

By default, the **is successful** option will be selected. Uncheck the option and select the **has timed out** option and click the **Done** button. This will change the arrow of that side of the parallel branch to a red-dashed line for the timeout.

To inform the user about the timeout, we'll use the **Post card in a chat or channel** action, posting as the flow bot in a chat (see *Figure 4.21*):

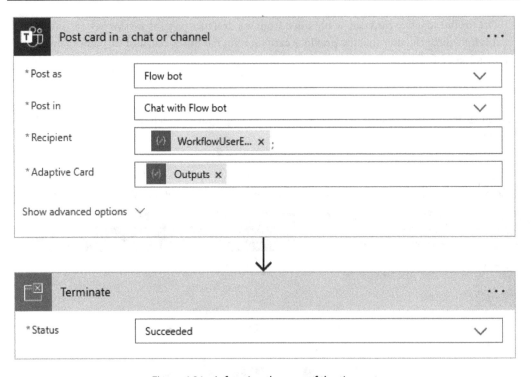

Figure 4.21 – Informing the user of the timeout

The recipient will be the same person we sent the previous message to, and the adaptive card will be the one we've created on this side of the parallel branch. Then, we can finish by adding a **Terminate** action with the status Succeeded. If we don't do that and the flow times out, it will appear to have failed in the flow history, and that could lead to misunderstandings.

Now let's see how the approvals look from beginning to end.

> **Note**
>
> Considering the flow as failed or successful when it times out is something that needs to be defined by each team when designing the solution. While I don't think it should appear as failed because the process has been handled correctly after informing the user, there may be some scenarios that might require it to appear as failed.

Managing the approval process on Teams

We have finished our Power Automate flow that manages purchase requisition approvals using Microsoft Teams. Now, what do the process and all these adaptive cards look like? Let's have a look. We can start by creating a new **Purchase Requisition** in F&O and submitting the workflow (see *Figure 4.22*):

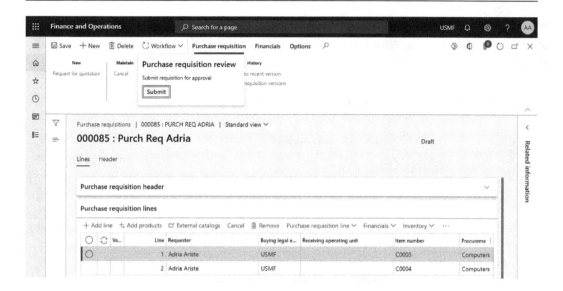

Figure 4.22 – Sending the purchase requisition for approval

You can see we're still using the standard Dynamics 365 F&O functionality. It's a simple purchase requisition with two lines that will be submitted for review using the standard purchase requisition workflow at the header level.

What happens behind the scenes? The workflow is submitted and the batch job that processes workflow messages will pick it up; that's when the business event will be emitted and our Power Automate flow will be started. Then, the flow bot will send us the adaptive card (see *Figure 4.23*):

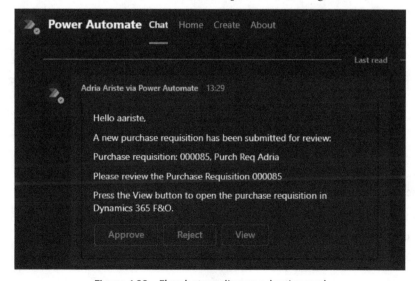

Figure 4.23 – Flow bot sending an adaptive card

We can see the text of the card, which is what we defined for the **Compose** actions, as well as the three buttons at the bottom. What happens if I reject the approval? You can go back to the F&O UI and check the workflow history (see *Figure 4.24*):

Figure 4.24 – Rejected workflow history

We can see it has been rejected and the message we added to the reject action appears. Let's recall it, change it so it can be approved, and submit it again. The flow bot will send us the card again, but this time I will approve it. Once the batch job picks it up, it will process the item and complete it (see *Figure 4.25*):

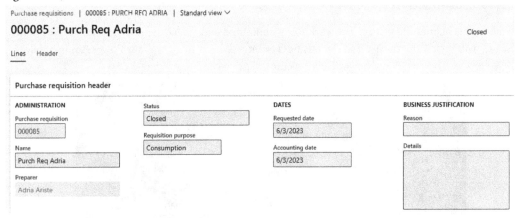

Figure 4.25 – Completed workflow

Our purchase requisition has been approved and is now **Closed**.

Finally, what happens when there's a timeout? What does it look like on Teams? What happens is we get the same card asking for approval or rejection (see *Figure 4.26*):

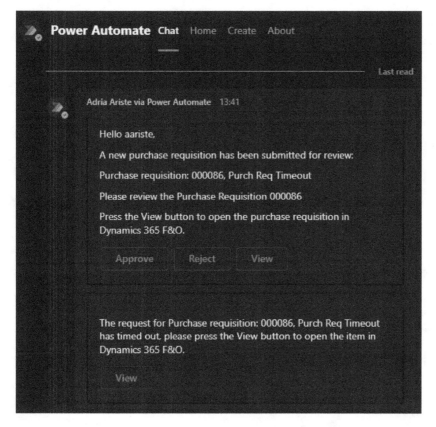

Figure 4.26 – Timed-out approval on Teams

Once the action times out, we get another message asking us to go into F&O to proceed with the approval. The **View** button provides a direct link to the record that needs to be approved.

In the following section, we'll learn how approvals can be done using emails instead of Teams messages.

Approvals using email

Approvals in Teams may not be a valid solution for everybody. Maybe you require a more asynchronous solution, such as emails. We can also accomplish something similar to what we did with Teams using Power Automate approvals.

> **Note**
>
> When using Power Automate approvals, an approval database will be provisioned in your Dataverse environment when you first add an approval to your flow and save it if it doesn't exist. You need to be at least an environment administrator to do this.

Our flow for this will look exactly the same up to the condition step, which checks whether the workflow can be processed (see *Figure 4.27*):

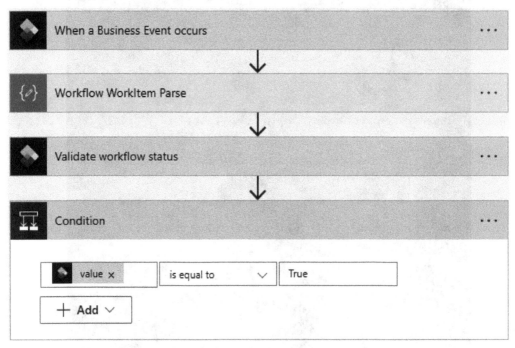

Figure 4.27 – Power Automate flow to process workflows

You can see the exact same steps here. So, to speed up development, you can save the flow that we created before as a new flow and remove everything from inside the **If yes** branch after the condition. That will be the basis for this section.

Adding Power Automate approvals

Now, inside the **If yes** branch, add the Start and wait for an approval action (see *Figure 4.28*):

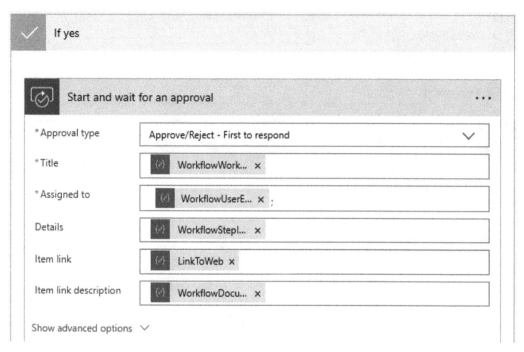

Figure 4.28 – Power Automate approval

The type will be **Approve/Reject - First to respond** because the Dynamics 365 F&O workflow will be the one managing the approvals if there's more than one approver. You can define a title yourself or use the `WorkflowWorkItemSubject` element from the trigger's output. Then, the **Assigned to** field should be set to `WorkflowUserEmail`, which we've used before. **Item link** should be set to the `LinkToWeb` element, which we also know already.

The next and final step will be adding an **Apply to each** action. This is required even if we only have one response because the output for the responses of the approval is an array; we need to loop through it even if it has a single element. The output used will be the `Responses` from the approval, and inside the loop, we will call the `WorkflowWorkItems-complete` action (see *Figure 4.29*):

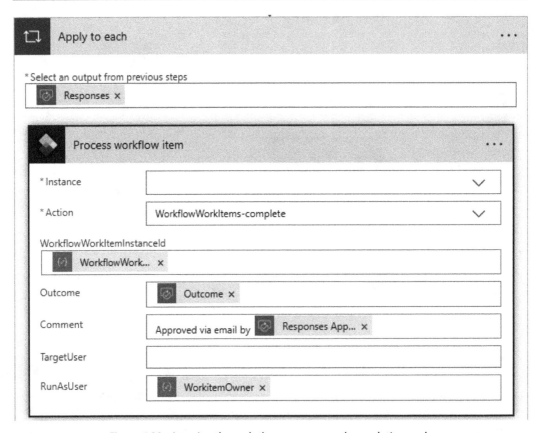

Figure 4.29 – Looping through the responses and completing each

In this scenario, we don't need to have an action for approvals and another one for rejections because we have the **Outcome** field in the **Responses**, which will be either approve or reject, and we can use it in the **Outcome** field of the complete action.

Once again, the `WorkflowWorkItemInstanceId` value will be the one that we get from the trigger output that has the same name. In the **RunAsUser** field, we need to use the value `WorkitemOwner`; otherwise, it'll fail.

Approving via email

When we create a new purchase requisition and submit it to the workflow, our Power Automate flow will be triggered exactly as in the Teams scenario. But this time, we will get an email (see *Figure 4.30*):

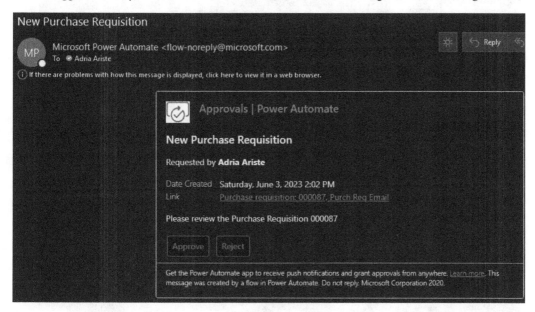

Figure 4.30 – Approval email

In the email, we have a link to the Dynamics 365 F&O record and two buttons to either approve or reject.

> **Note**
>
> If you're using the Teams approvals app, you will also receive a message about the approval in Teams.

This time, I will approve the requisition right away, and when I click the **Approve** button, a comments section appears (see *Figure 4.31*):

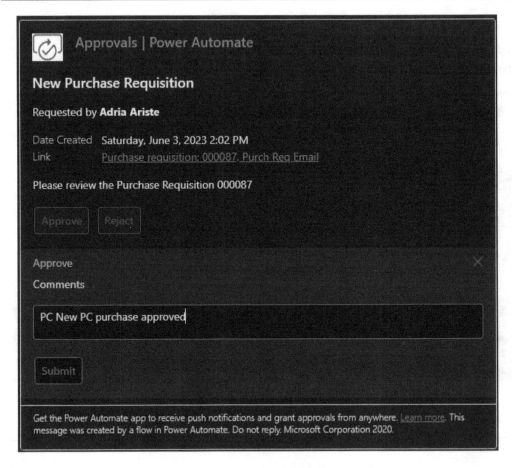

Figure 4.31 – Comments for the email approval

This is something that the previous scenario doesn't have and that can be very useful, especially when rejecting workflows. You can provide a reason or ask for more details. If you use the **Responses Comments** value in the **Comments** field when processing the approval, you will get those comments in the F&O workflow history too.

Summary

In this chapter, we learned how to use Microsoft Power Automate to manage Dynamics 365 F&O workflow approvals using Microsoft Teams. We discovered how to customize an adaptive card and post it via the flow bot to a Teams channel or chat, how to define a timeout for this action, and how to process the workflow elements and manage the timeout outcome.

We also saw how to use parallel branches, one for managing the response from Teams and another for processing a timeout.

Finally, we dived into the implementation of more asynchronous approvals using emails through Power Automate, added Power Automate approvals within the flow, and processed responses via email.

In the next chapter, we will learn how to use Power Automate to connect to an SFTP server instead of using X++ to create a connection to an SFTP server and retrieve or upload files.

Questions

Here are some questions to test your understanding of the chapter. The answers to the questions are given at the end.

1. What tool in Microsoft Power Automate is used to post an adaptive card to a Teams channel or chat?

    a. Post a text card and wait for a response

    b. Post adaptive card and wait for a response

    c. Post adaptive card and do not wait for a response

    d. None of the above

2. In the described approval workflow, what happens if no response is given within the 15-minute timeout?

    a. The process automatically approves the request

    b. The process automatically rejects the request

    c. A timeout notification is sent to the user with a link to the record needing approval

    d. The workflow stops and needs to be restarted

3. What is the purpose of creating a parallel branch in this approval workflow?

    a. To manage the response from Teams and to process a timeout

    b. To send multiple adaptive cards to different users

    c. To duplicate the workflow for backup

    d. To process both approval and rejection simultaneously

4. How does the user receive notification for approval or rejection in Teams?

    a. Via an adaptive card posted by the flow bot

    b. Via an email from the flow bot

    c. Via a pop-up notification from Teams

    d. Via a text message from Teams

5. When implementing asynchronous approvals through Power Automate, what additional feature is available to users?

    a. The ability to add attachments to the approval or rejection response

    b. The ability to add comments for additional context or information

    c. The ability to extend the timeout duration

    d. The ability to approve or reject via a voice command

Further reading

To know more about replacing F&O processes with Power Automate, you can visit the following links:

Add a condition to a cloud flow:

`https://learn.microsoft.com/en-us/power-automate/add-condition`

Parallel branches:

`https://powerautomate.microsoft.com/en-us/blog/parallel-actions/`

Get started with approvals:

`https://learn.microsoft.com/en-us/power-automate/get-started-approvals`

Power Automate Approvals Provisioning Overview and Troubleshooting:

`https://support.microsoft.com/en-us/topic/power-automate-approvals-provisioning-overview-and-troubleshooting-2306313a-49fa-efde-c716-a34c573ec942`

Answers

1. a. Post adaptive card and wait for a response

2. c. A timeout notification is sent to the user with a link to the record needing approval

3. a. To manage the response from Teams and to process a timeout

4. a. Via an adaptive card posted by the flow bot

5. b. The ability to add comments for additional context or information

5

Building Automations and Integrations

We're used to creating integrations inside Dynamics 365 **Finance and Operations (F&O)** using X++ and automating the process execution using batches. What if I told you we can also achieve that outside F&O? Let's learn how to use Power Automate flows to connect to an **FTP/SFTP server** to retrieve a file and update a field in F&O. FTP access from within X++ is discouraged since the architecture moved from a classic monolith to Service Fabric containers, and Power Automate can help us solve this scenario.

To demonstrate this, we will use a scheduled cloud flow to download a file from an SFTP server. This file will be a JSON file that contains a list of customers and their customer groups, and we will use it to update the value of the customer group if it's different than the existing one.

In this chapter, we'll learn about the following:

- The issue with FTP and self-service deployments
- Connecting to an FTP server in Power Automate
- Parsing a JSON file
- Using the F&O connector to update a record
- Using the Dataverse connector to update a record

Technical requirements

If you followed the setup steps in the previous chapters, you should have all the necessary technical requirements.

Additionally, you will need access to an FTP server where you will host the JSON file.

You can find a `.axpp` file containing the elements that have been created for this chapter in this book's GitHub repository: `https://github.com/PacktPublishing/Extending-D365-Finance-and-Operation-apps-with-Power-Platform-/tree/main/Chapter%2006`.

The issue with FTP and self-service deployments

Even though using FTP or SFTP servers when building integrations might seem a bit outdated, it's a common scenario. Many third parties, especially banks, still use them to distribute information instead of building APIs.

In the past, we could create this integration using X++ and some .NET to connect to an FTP server and operate it. Similarly, for an SFTP server, we used SSH.NET.

However, some issues tended to appear after the change to the new self-service deployments, which moved the infrastructure from a classic monolithic architecture to a container-based one. The authentication request sent from F&O to the FTP server could have a different IP address than the request to access a file or folder, and an error would occur, breaking the integration.

> **Note**
> If you develop a solution to connect to an FTP server using X++ and test it successfully in a development environment, you must know that there's no guarantee that it'll work when deployed to a sandbox or production environment. The dev VM infrastructure is different, so you won't have the issue described here.

The solution

What can we do to avoid this issue? We can use a Power Automate cloud flow to connect to the FTP server!

Depending on what type of server you are connecting to, you will use the FTP or SFTP – SSH connectors. Both connectors are very similar regarding the required parameters, but the SFTP – SSH one has more security-related options.

> **FTP versus SFTP**
> FTP and SFTP are both protocols designed for transferring files, but they have different security features and use cases. FTP is older and transmits data in an unencrypted form. SFTP is part of the SSH protocol, which encrypts the data during transfer, ensuring a much higher level of security. This makes SFTP more suitable for transferring sensitive or confidential data.

In this example, we will use the FTP connector. In the next section, we'll learn how to configure it. If you have to use an SFTP server instead, you need to complete the required parameters in the connection setup.

Implementing this solution using Power Automate instead of X++ provides several benefits, with one of the most notable being decoupling, as we've seen in previous chapters. This makes the system more adaptable to changes. With Power Automate, you can create and modify workflows easily without having to change the underlying code base. This results in fewer dependencies and reduces the risk of unintentionally affecting other parts of the system when making changes in X++.

Another benefit of using Power Automate is the increase in development speed. Power Automate offers a user-friendly drag-and-drop interface, which can significantly reduce the development time compared to writing code in X++. This also makes it more accessible to individuals who may not have extensive coding experience, expanding the pool of contributors to the project. It also enables rapid prototyping and iteration, which is especially beneficial in environments where business processes are dynamic and need to be adjusted frequently.

Connecting to an FTP server in Power Automate

The flow in this example will run daily on a schedule and retrieve a JSON file with customer information. We will use the contents of the file to update the customer groups when there is a change. So, let's start by creating a new scheduled cloud flow (see *Figure 5.1*):

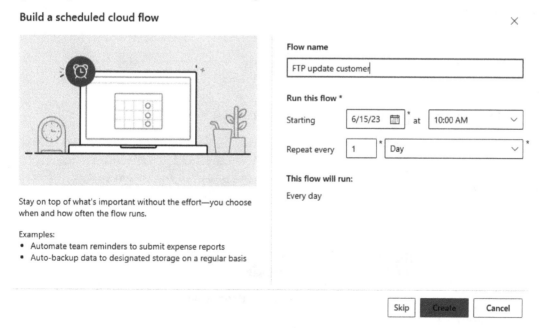

Figure 5.1 – Creating a scheduled cloud flow

Ensure that the flow repeats once a day and select the time when the flow should run. In my case, the flow will run daily at 10:00 A.M.

Now, add a new action and look for the FTP connector. Then, select **Get file content**. After adding the connector, we must configure the connection to the FTP server (see *Figure 5.2*):

Figure 5.2 – Setting up an FTP connection

We need to give this connection a name and add the FTP address, username, and password. Once we click the **Create** button, we will be able to select the file we want to retrieve (see *Figure 5.3*):

Figure 5.3 – Navigating the FTP folders

Navigate to the folder containing the file and select it. This action will return the content of the file encoded in a `base64` string.

Using the SFTP connector

Before continuing, we'll take a quick look at the SFTP connector (see *Figure 5.4*):

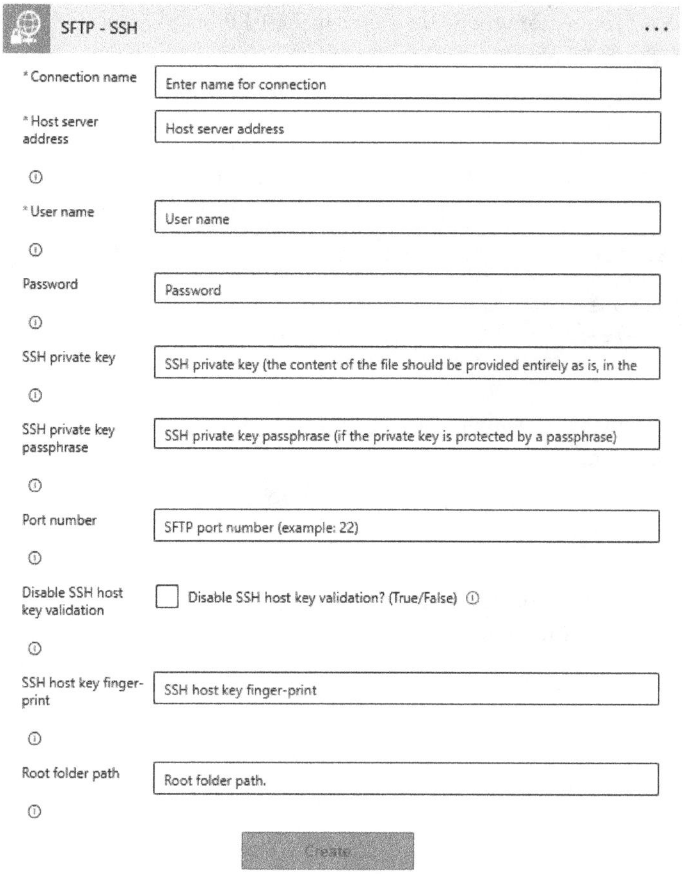

Figure 5.4 – The SFTP connector

As we can see, some of the fields are the same. However, some fields, such as the password, are not mandatory. This might surprise you if you've never worked with SFTP servers, but there's a reason for this.

When authenticating to an SFTP server, you can use different authentication methods, depending on its setup:

- **Password authentication**: Like with the FTP connector, we can authenticate using a username and password.

- **Public key authentication**: This method uses a pair of keys – a public key and a private key – plus the username, and optionally a password for the private key (not the user). The public key is configured in the server, and we use the private key to authenticate.

These are the ones we can use in the connector, but other methods exist, such as keyboard-interactive authentication, host-based authentication, or Kerberos, a protocol that only works for Windows.

The output of the SFTP connector will be the same as the FTP one. The file, which is encoded in a base64 string inside a JSON object, will look like this:

```
{
    "$content-type": "application/octet-stream",
    "$content": "WwogICAgewogICAgICAgICJkYXRhQXJlYUlkIjogIlVTTUYi-
LAogICAgICAgICJjdXN0b21lck51bWJlciI6ICJVUy0wMDEiLAogICAgICAgICJjdX-
N0b21lckdyb3VwSWQiOiAiMzAiCiAgICB9LAogICAgewogICAgICAgICJkYXRhQXJlY-
UlkIjogIlVTTUYiLAogICAgICAgICJjdXN0b21lck51bWJlciI6ICJVUy0wMDIiLAogI-
CAgICAgICJjdXN0b21lckdyb3VwSWQiOiAiMzAiCiAgICB9LAogICAgewogICAgICAgIC-
JkYXRhQXJlYUlkIjogIlVTTUYiLAogICAgICAgICJjdXN0b21lck51bWJlciI6ICJVUy-
0wMDMiLAogICAgICAgICJjdXN0b21lckdyb3VwSWQiOiAiMTAiCiAgICB9Cl0K"
}
```

Now that we have the content, we will proceed to convert it into a string, decoding the base64 text of the $content member.

Parsing a JSON file

To start, we need to convert the base64 string into a human-readable version. Thankfully, Power Platform offers some built-in functions that allow us to decode and encode base64.

Add a new **Compose** block and change to the **Expression** tab (see *Figure 5.5*):

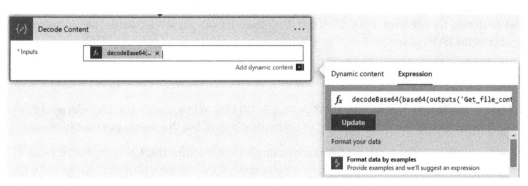

Figure 5.5 – Power Automate expression editor

First, add the decodeBase64 function, then the base64 function, since we need to understand that the content is not just a string but an encoded base64 text. Finally, change to the **Dynamic content** tab and click on the **File Content** output of your FTP connector. The full line should look like this:

```
decodeBase64(base64(outputs('Get_file_content')?['body']))
```

In this formula, the Get_file_content piece is equal to the name of the FTP action that retrieves the file.

This will return the content of the file, which for this example is as follows:

```
[
    {
        "dataAreaId": "USMF",
        "customerNumber": "US-001",
        "customerGroupId": "10"
    },
    {
        "dataAreaId": "USMF",
        "customerNumber": "US-002",
        "customerGroupId": "30"
    },
    {
        "dataAreaId": "USMF",
        "customerNumber": "US-003",
        "customerGroupId": "10"
    }
]
```

This is what the JSON file looks like. It's a JSON array that contains three entries, each of which provides information about the company (dataAreaId), customer account number (customerNumber), and the customer group (customerGroupId).

After all of this, we will have some JSON text. Let's learn how to parse it so that we can access each member of the JSON object.

Why parse?

In previous chapters, we learned a bit about parsing JSON files. Why are we doing this? We could skip this and access each of the elements using the expression editor, but that would be prone to errors.

The other reason is that we want our future selves, or whoever is editing the flow in the future, to have a better experience if they need to do it. Parsing the content of a JSON file will make us happy and will also allow us to access the value of dataAreaId, customerNumber, or customerGroupId individually in the **Dynamic content** tab.

Add a new action and look for **Parse JSON** (see *Figure 5.6*):

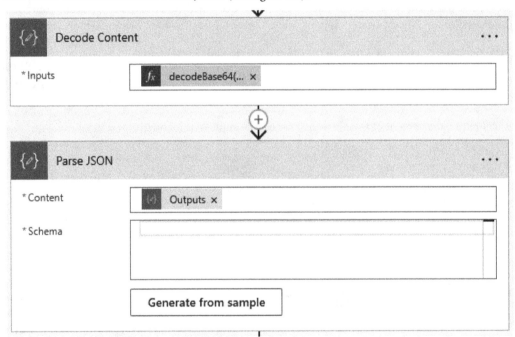

Figure 5.6 – The Decode Content and Parse JSON blocks

We'll select the output of the **Decode Content** block we created before as the content of the parse JSON action. Now, we need to define the schema. A JSON schema is a way of defining and validating the structure of JSON data, as well as specifying data types, formats, and other constraints.

We can create the schema by hand, but that's not optimal. We can do this faster using an example of the JSON file we want to parse. Copy the content of the file we've seen before and click on the **Generate from sample** button at the bottom of the parse action. A new dialogue will open (see *Figure 5.7*):

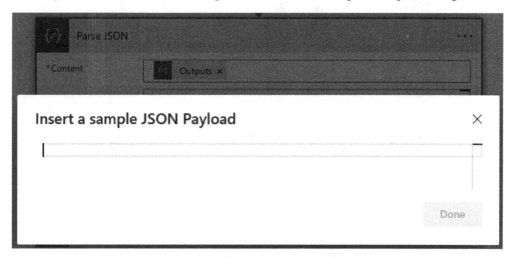

Figure 5.7 – JSON payload to generate the schema

In this new dialogue, paste the content we copied and click the **Done** button. This will generate the schema automatically.

If you take a look at the generated schema, you will see that it tells us the following:

- The JSON file is an array
- Each array has three properties of type string
- All three properties are essential

> **Note**
>
> If any of the properties in the JSON object were not mandatory, such as if `customerGroupId` did not need to be informed in any of the items, then we would have the option of making the `customerGroupId` property optional or not required.

Now, thanks to parsing, we can select the different properties in the **Dynamic content** window (see *Figure 5.8*):

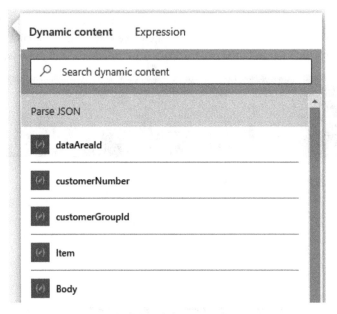

Figure 5.8 – Individual elements after parsing

Here, we can see the **dataAreaId**, **customerNumber,** and **customerGroupId** elements and select them with ease.

Now that we have all the data, let's update the records in F&O.

Using the F&O connector to update a record

We can't update the records straight away. Remember that the JSON file is an array, so we need to loop through the items in the array to process each one. Add an **Apply to each** control block (see *Figure 5.9*):

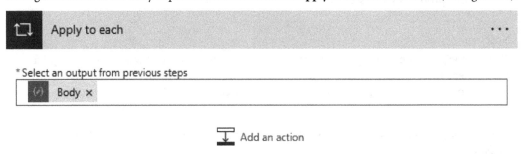

Figure 5.9 – The Apply to each control block

In this control block, we must select the **Body** element of the parse JSON action. The body contains the JSON array we need to loop through. All the actions we add inside this block will be repeated for each item of the array.

Next, we will process each record – first selecting it and then updating the record if we need to.

Getting the existing record

Remember that to update a record in Power Automate using the F&O connector, we have to select it. This is similar to what we do in X++ – we need to do a `select forupdate` first, and then update it.

To do that, we will use the **Get a record** action of the Fin & Ops Apps connector (see *Figure 5.10*):

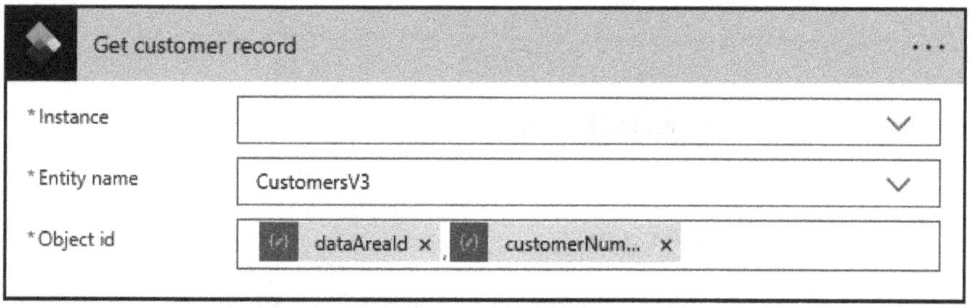

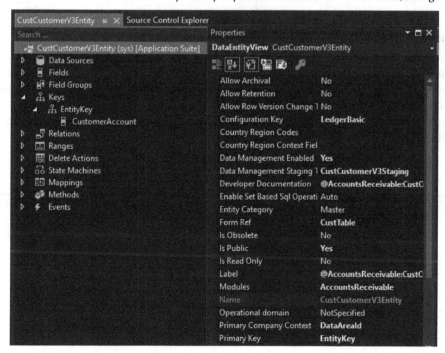

Figure 5.10 – The Get a record action

Select the instance you're working on, and then the `CustomersV3` entity. Then, in the **Object id** field, we must add all the fields of the data entity's entity key. We can check this on the AOT (see *Figure 5.11*):

Figure 5.11 – Data entity properties in Visual Studio

If we open the **EntityKey** node under **Keys**, we'll see that there's only one field – **CustomerAccount**. But just adding that to the **Object id** field of the flow action wouldn't work! Why? We still need the company. If we check the **Primary Company Context** property of the data entity, we will see that **DataAreaId** is specified there. This means that the main backing table of the data entity is saving data per company, and we need to add the `dataAreaId` field to **Object id** in Power Automate. For example, the customer table (`CustTable`) saves data per company, and each company has different customers. On the other hand, the global address book table (`DirPartyTable` and all the ones inheriting from it) will display the same data in all companies because it doesn't store data per company.

> **Note**
>
> The **Object id** fields must be separated by a comma (,).

Adding conditional branches

Once we have the record, we can check if the customer group value from the JSON file is the same as the records'. Couldn't we just update the record even if the values were the same? Yes, that wouldn't be an issue, but in the process, we're making unnecessary calls to the ERP and we should avoid that. Another thing we want to avoid is triggering unwanted updates, such as creating primary addresses each time we update a record using the CustomersV2 entity.

> **Not just performance**
>
> When designing integrations, regardless of whether you're using Power Automate flows or other tools to interact with F&O, it is a best practice to reduce calls to the ERP. This is not only done for performance-related reasons! On the Dataverse/CRM side, entitlement limits exist; you have a limited amount of daily API calls and if you go over that limit, you might need to add capacity add-ons to the users. This is something we don't have in F&O yet but could come in the future.

Now, add a new conditional control block to compare the values of the customer groups (see *Figure 5.12*):

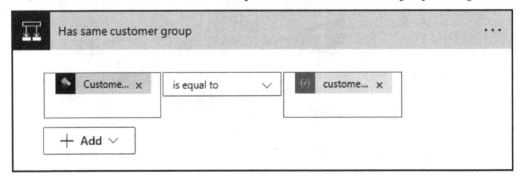

Figure 5.12 – Conditional block

You can add the value from the parsed JSON file and the value from the retrieved record to any of the sides; the comparison operation will be the same. We're comparing if the values are equal, so on the **If yes** branch, we'll take no further action.

In the **If no** branch, which means that the values are different, we will add an **Update a record** F&O Apps action (see *Figure 5.13*):

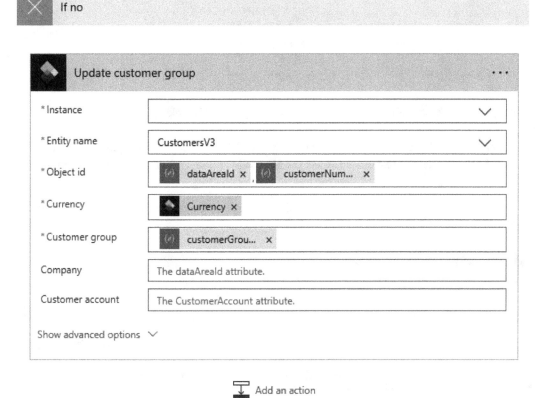

Figure 5.13 – An If no branch with an update action

Once again, we must select the instance and the CustomersV3 data entity. As we did with the **Get a record** action, we have to add the entity key values in the **Object id** field. Finally, we must complete all the mandatory fields marked with a red asterisk. By coincidence, the customer group is one of them!

Our flow is ready, and we can test it without waiting for the scheduled time to trigger – thanks to the test functionality of the designer. The customers we're updating are US-001, US-002, and US-003 of the USMF company (we're using the Contoso demo data), which have the customer groups 30, 30, and 10, respectively:

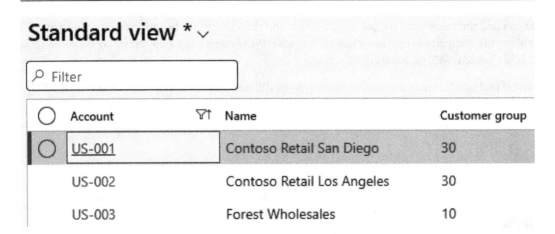

Figure 5.14 – Updated customers in the JSON file

The contents of the file will only update the first customer, US-001, and set its customer group to 10. Let's run the flow! Click the **Test** button, select the **Manually** option, and click the **Test** and **Run flow** buttons. Close the dialogue and wait for the flow to finish executing.

You should have green checks on all the steps of the flow. Go back to the customer form in F&O and refresh it (see *Figure 5.15*):

Standard view * ⌄

🔍 Filter

	Account	▽↑ Name	Customer group
◯	US-001	Contoso Retail San Diego	10
	US-002	Contoso Retail Los Angeles	30
	US-003	Forest Wholesales	10

Figure 5.15 – US-001 customer with a new customer group

As we can see, US-001 has been updated. Of course, I could've changed it by hand. So, let's look at the loop to see what happened to each customer, depending on the value of the customer group we got from the JSON file in the FTP (see *Figure 5.16*):

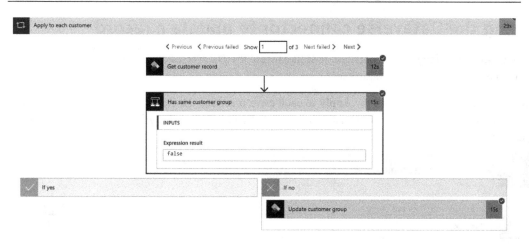

Figure 5.16 – US-001 has been updated

In the first item, which corresponds to US-001, the comparison is false, so the record is updated in the **If no** branch.

For US-002 and US-003, the comparison is true. This is because the customer groups are equal (see *Figure 5.17*):

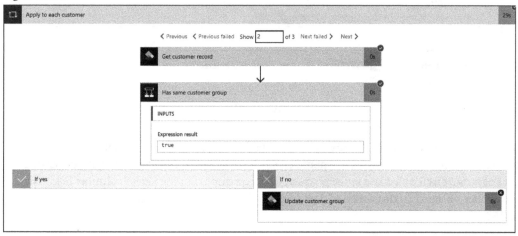

Figure 5.17 – US-002 and US-003 haven't been updated

We can see a cross on the **If no** branch's update action. This means it has not run because the evaluation of the comparison returned true.

So far, we've only used the F&O connector. Let's learn how we can do the same using the Dataverse connector.

Using the Dataverse connector to update a record

What if, instead of the F&O connector, we'd like to use the Dataverse connector and take advantage of the F&O virtual tables in Dataverse?

The flow will be the same until the **Apply to each customer** loop. However, everything inside it will look different due to how the Dataverse actions work. Inside the loop, we will add a **List rows** action (see *Figure 5.18*):

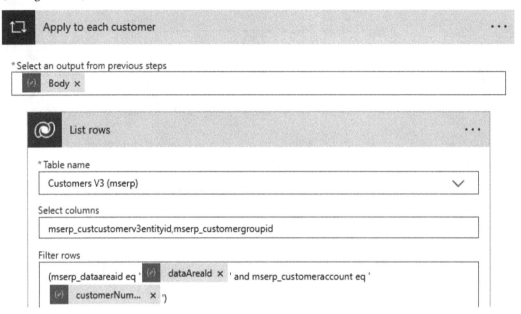

Figure 5.18 – List rows

We will select the **Customers V3 (mserp)** virtual table. Remember that if it's not appearing in the list, it's because it's not enabled. So, we should enable it, as we saw in *Chapter 2*. We will add mserp_customerv3entityid and mserp_customergroupid to the **Select columns** field. Then, we will filter on mserp_dataareaid and mserp_customeraccount using the values from the JSON file.

> **XrmToolBox and Dataverse REST Builder**
>
> When working with Dataverse and to create the filter expressions faster, I recommend using XrmToolBox and the Dataverse REST Builder tool. XrmToolBox is a Windows app that connects to Dataverse, and it contains tools created by the community. Dataverse REST Builder allows you to create a REST call to a table, add filters, sort by or select the fields, and see it in different formats, including Power Automate, so that you can use it later.

This operation will return a set of records, even if it's only returning a single record. This means we need to loop through the result of the list rows action. Add another **Apply to each** control element. For the input, select the `value` field of the previous step (see *Figure 5.19*):

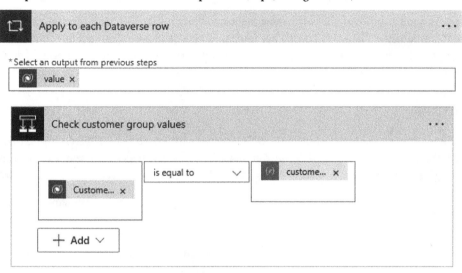

Figure 5.19 – Looping through the List rows items

As we did with the F&O connector, add a conditional control block where we compare the value we get from the JSON file and the current item of the loop.

As we saw earlier, the **If yes** branch has no outcomes. In the **If no** branch, we will add an **Update a row** action (see *Figure 5.20*):

Figure 5.20 – Update a row

Here, we will select **Customers V3** (mserp) under **Table name**, select the `mserp_customerv3entityid` field we selected in the list step for **Row ID**, and add the value from the JSON file in the **Customer group** field.

The result of running this flow will be the same as the one that uses the F&O Apps connector. Because the output contains the **List rows** actions, we must add an extra loop. Although this might not be the most optimal way of doing it, I wanted to demonstrate that we can use both connectors and get the same result!

Summary

In this chapter, we learned how to integrate an FTP server with Dynamics 365 F&O through Power Automate. We started by setting up a Power Automate flow that gets triggered at specific intervals to monitor an FTP server for new or modified files. When the trigger is activated, it retrieves a JSON file.

Next, we learned how to parse and process the JSON data to update records in Dynamics 365 F&O. This involves using a loop to iterate through each item in the JSON array, retrieving existing records, and comparing the data. To ensure consistency, we should check whether differences are found between the JSON data and the existing records using the F&O Apps connector to update the record.

Finally, we learned how to use the Dataverse connector to update records. We saw that this method, although slightly less optimal due to an extra loop, achieves the same result as the F&O connector.

Thanks to Power Automate, we can create integrations that we used to do in X++. This can also help decouple some processes, and thanks to how quickly we can incorporate changes in Power Automate flows, we can change processes faster.

In the next chapter, we'll start learning about Power Apps and how they can serve us as Dynamics 365 F&O consultants.

Questions

Answer the following questions to test your knowledge of this chapter. You will find the answers at the end of the chapter.

1. What is the source of the file we will use?

    a. An email

    b. Dynamics 365 F&O

    c. An FTP server

    d. A database

2.   What control is used to iterate through each item in the JSON array from the FTP server?

    a.   **Select each**

    b.   **Iterate through**

    c.   **Apply to each**

    d.   **Loop through**

3.   Why is reducing calls to F&O a best practice?

    a.   It improves security

    b.   It ensures data accuracy

    c.   It lets us stay within API call limits and improve performance

    d.   It enables real-time data processing

4.   Which action in the F&O Apps connector is used to update a record in Dynamics 365 F&O?

    a.   Modify a record

    b.   Update a record

    c.   Change a record

    d.   Amend a record

5.   What alternative connector was mentioned in this chapter for updating records in Dynamics 365 F&O?

    a.   FTP

    b.   Dynamics 365

    c.   Dataverse

    d.   Azure Blob Storage

Further reading

To learn more about the topics that were covered in this chapter, take a look at the following resources:

Self-service deployment overview: `https://learn.microsoft.com/en-us/dynamics365/fin-ops-core/dev-itpro/deployment/infrastructure-stack`

Known issues with self-service deployment: `https://learn.microsoft.com/en-us/dynamics365/fin-ops-core/dev-itpro/deployment/known-issues-new-deployment-experience#ftp`

Run flows on a schedule: `https://learn.microsoft.com/en-us/power-automate/run-scheduled-tasks`

Apply to each action: `https://learn.microsoft.com/en-us/power-automate/apply-to-each`

Add a condition to a flow: `https://learn.microsoft.com/en-us/power-automate/add-condition`

XrmToolBox: `https://www.xrmtoolbox.com/`

Dataverse REST Builder: `https://www.xrmtoolbox.com/plugins/GuidoPreite.DRB/`

Answers

1. c. An FTP server
2. c. Apply to each
3. c. It lets us stay within API call limits and improve performance
4. b. Update a record
5. c. Dataverse

6

Power Apps: What's in it for Finance and Operations Consultants?

In this chapter, we'll delve into the heart of Power Apps and what we can do with it and the Dynamics 365 finance and operations apps. We will learn about the different types of apps in Power Apps, such as model-driven apps and canvas apps. We will also see how we can open an app from the **Dynamics 365 for Finance and Operations (F&O)** user interface.

In this chapter, we'll learn about the following:

- Model-driven and canvas apps
- Embedding a Power Apps app in a finance and operations form

Technical requirements

If you have gone through the steps in *Chapter 5*, you should have all technical requirements completed.

The F&O objects used for the demos in the following pages can be found at `https://github.com/PacktPublishing/Extending-D365-Finance-and-Operation-apps-with-Power-Platform-/tree/main/Chapter%2006`.

Model-driven and canvas apps

Power Apps is Microsoft's low-code platform that enables us to build custom apps on top of Dataverse. Power Apps also has the same connector concept as Power Automate, and thanks to the connectors, we can use data and services not only from Microsoft but also from other vendors.

Maybe when we talk about apps, the first thing that comes to our minds is mobile apps, the ones you have on your phone. And, while it's true that you can create mobile applications using Power Apps, you can also create other formats to play the apps on a tablet or even in a full-screen web browser.

> **Power Apps in a browser is not Power Pages!**
>
> In the past, when Power Pages was released as Power Apps Portals, a portal was a different type of Power App. Full-screen Power Apps is not to be confused with Power Pages; it's just Power Apps being displayed on a browser.

Remember, Power Apps is used to build custom applications, and Power Pages is used to build public-facing web pages. Additionally, Power Pages has its own maker portal to create portals just as Power Apps has its own portal to make applications. Now, you may ask yourself why we would need to create external apps if Dynamics 365 F&O is already a web-based ERP. That's a good question, one that many of us have thought about. And the answer is like the one given when we ask something like this when using Power Automate.

As always, we must analyze the business scenario we're trying to solve. And, while the ERP is web-based and has a responsive version that looks fine on a mobile phone screen, I think we can agree that it's not made to be displayed on a phone screen.

Imagine a salesperson who is visiting their customers and needs to check the on-hand of a particular item and aren't carrying their laptop with them. What should they do? They can go into the ERP with their mobile device, go to the released products form, select the product, and check the current on-hand inventory. *Figure 6.1* is what they'd see:

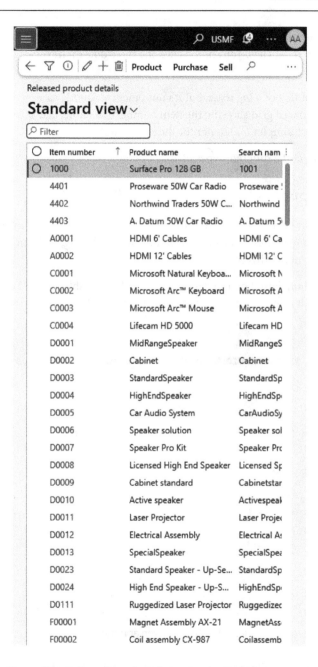

Figure 6.1 – Released products form on a vertical phone screen

We can see the grid with the released products list quite well, but look at the size of the scrolling bars, especially the horizontal scrolling bar. F&O grids usually show a lot of information in master forms, much like the one for products; and that's not ideal for phone screens.

And there's another issue: the on-hand form is accessed from the **Manage inventory** submenu, which is not displayed in the vertical view. You should click the three dots in the top-right corner to display the hidden submenus.

We could do this; it's not that of a big issue, but it's not practical. In this case, we could create an app in Power Apps with a reduced grid showing the item number, the name, and a link to see its on-hand inventory. That'd be much simpler and better for the sales team!

Now, let's learn a bit about the different types of apps in Power Apps that exist.

Model-driven apps

We will start with a short overview of model-driven apps. If you've ever used the CRM products of Dynamics 365, such as Dynamics 365 Sales, Dynamics 365 Marketing, or Dynamics 365 Customer Service, their forms are model-driven apps.

Model-driven apps are built based on the data model. You have a table and will create forms, views, or dashboards based on it using an app designer inside the Power Apps maker portal (see *Figure 6.2*):

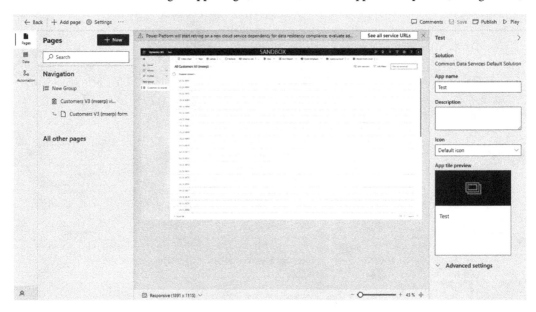

Figure 6.2 – Model-driven app designer

For the design, we can select different data sources and components, add pages, and customize each page with different components. It's also possible to add business process flows to the apps in order to guide users' steps.

These kinds of apps can have a data source that uses an F&O virtual table to display data from the ERP in Dataverse. However, we will not focus on them because almost all the apps that we will create will be canvas apps. We will discuss how we can embed and use these apps with F&O data.

Canvas apps

If you already know a bit about Power Apps, it's possible that canvas apps are the first things that come to mind.

Canvas apps are a way of creating applications without writing code and using a drag-and-drop method that lets you place elements onto the app canvas; hence the name (see *Figure 6.3*):

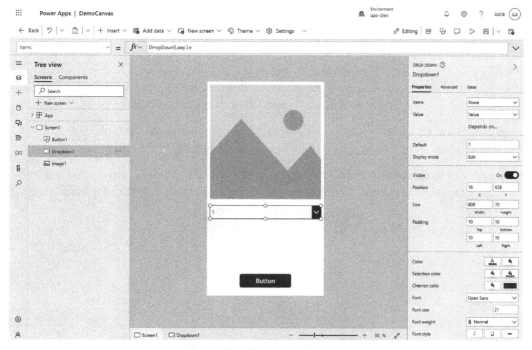

Figure 6.3 – Canvas app designer

Once a new element is added to the canvas app, we can place it wherever we want, either by clicking and dragging it or using the properties on the right pane.

The designer is divided into the following three parts:

- **Left side panes**: These show the details of the screens and elements of the app, data sources, Power Automate flows, media, and variables

- **Center pane**: This is the designer of the app

- **Right pane**: Like the Visual Studio properties pane, we can see and edit the properties of the selected element here

Additionally, there's a formula bar at the top consisting of a drop-down control and the formula bar itself. In the drop-down control, we can select different properties and actions depending on the control that's selected. In the bar, we can change the behavior of the selected element or action. We will learn more about this in the next chapters!

> **Note**
>
> We won't be covering it in this book, but let me explain a bit about Power Fx. Power Fx is a new component of the Power Platform. It is a low-code programming language that allows users to use expression-based formulas, like those used in Excel, which makes it accessible to a wide range of users. It's used in Power Apps for defining logic, manipulating data, or interacting with data sources.

For most of the properties that a control or app element has, we can change them using the property pane on the right side of the screen or the formula bar at the top.

We will be able to add components to the app, such as text input boxes, drop-down menus, buttons, images, AI builder elements, and more. Those will appear in the left pane and can be renamed, grouped, and reorganized. In the right pane, change its properties to meet our requirements.

As well as in Power Automate, thanks to the connectors, we can add data sources from many different services in addition to the data we have in tables and virtual tables in Dataverse.

Canvas apps can be executed in a web browser, in the iOS or Android Power Apps application (see *Figure 6.4*), or as a standalone native application for iOS or Android thanks to the wrap functionality.

Figure 6.4 – Power Apps Android app

When you use the Android or iOS app to run a Power Apps app from your mobile device, the app is run in an embedded way inside the native app on the device.

> **Wrap**
>
> To use the wrap functionality, you'll have to take some steps that may require registering on the Android or iOS developer platforms and using a Mac device to sign the app.

Regarding F&O, we can embed a Power Apps app in a form. In the next section, we will learn the two ways we have to do this.

Embedding a Power Apps app in a finance and operations form

There are some scenarios where we can extend the functionality in F&O using a Power Apps app inside F&O. Not only do we embed the app, we can also complement F&O with a Power Apps app, which uses data from F&O.

Next, we're going to learn how we can let the Power Apps app know which record in F&O to use to show the corresponding data in the app.

Passing the app context

What is exactly the app context? When we embed a Power Apps app inside Dynamics 365 F&O, we expect it to show us the relevant data depending on the active F&O record. So, if, for example, we embed an app that displays the open transactions of a customer in the customer's form, we would expect to see only the transactions of the customer that we have selected.

We can achieve that thanks to two variables that are passed from F&O to Power Apps:

- `EntityId`: When we embed the app in a form, we select the field that is passed to Power Apps—this will be the `EntityId`
- `cmp`: This is the current legal entity in F&O

And how do we accomplish this? We need to define two variables in the Power Apps app. For example, in the `OnStart` method of the app we need to add this formula:

```
If(!IsBlank(Param("EntityId")), Set(FinOpsInput, Param("EntityId")),
Set(FinOpsInput, ""));

If(!IsBlank(Param("cmp")), Set(FinOpsLegalEntity, Param("cmp")),
Set(FinOpsLegalEntity, ""));
```

The `Param("EntityId")` and `Param("cmp")` parameters are what are retrieved from the context and shouldn't be changed. The `FinOpsInput` and `FinOpsLegalEntity` are the variables that are created in the `OnStart` method and store the values that the `Param` gets. The variable names can be changed to suit your needs.

Let's see a quick and simple example of how this is done. I've created a blank canvas app and added the code in the `OnStart` method (*see Figure 6.5*):

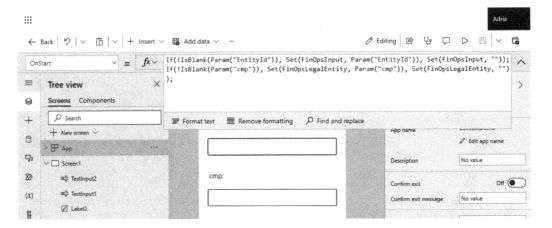

Figure 6.5 – OnStart method with context formula

On the **Tree view** panel, we've selected the **App** node, and then on the **Property selector**, we select the `OnStart` method. Finally, we paste the code into the formula bar. This will be enough to declare and create the variables and set their value when the app starts.

Next, I will add two labels to the app and two text boxes (see *Figure 6.6*):

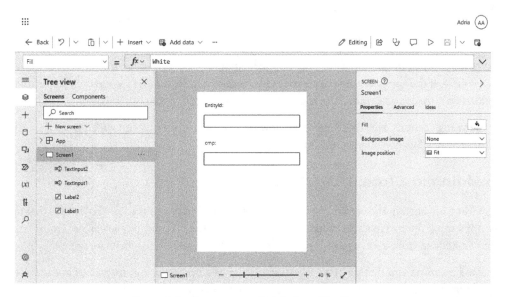

Figure 6.6 – Canvas app with labels and text boxes

There's a label for the `EntityId` parameter and another one for the `cmp` parameter, and there are two text boxes where the values that come from Dynamics 365 F&O will be displayed.

Now we can go to the customers form in F&O and open the embedded app, which I've configured to use the account number as the context (see *Figure 6.7*):

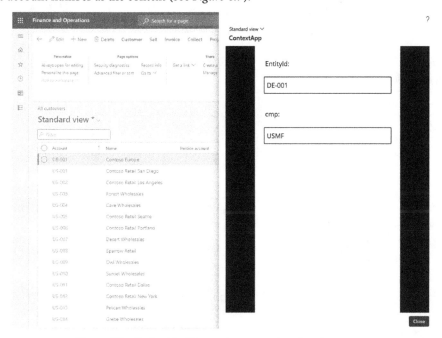

Figure 6.7 – Embedded Power Apps app showing the context

We can see that in the F&O form we're in the DE-001 customer record, and the app is showing that same value in the EntityId parameter. The company in this case is the USMF one.

Thanks to the context, we can show meaningful information of F&O's active records in a canvas Power App. Of course, if the app needs no context because it's meant to be used as a standalone application but inside F&O, we can just embed the app and forget about the context.

In the following sections, we will see in detail how the Power Apps app is embedded from the form UI or using Visual Studio and customization.

Embedding in a form from the UI

The app we've just seen in the previous section has been embedded from the UI. You can see that the Power Apps app is opened in a sort of modal form that leaves the F&O form unavailable. This is what the apps embedded from a form in the Dynamics 365 UI look like. Let's see how it's done.

I've created a canvas app that displays the attachments of a customer. So, instead of going to the standard attachment form in F&O, we can open the embedded app and see them in it.

In the customer form, we need to click the Power Apps icon on the top-right corner and click the **Add an app** button (see *Figure 6.8*):

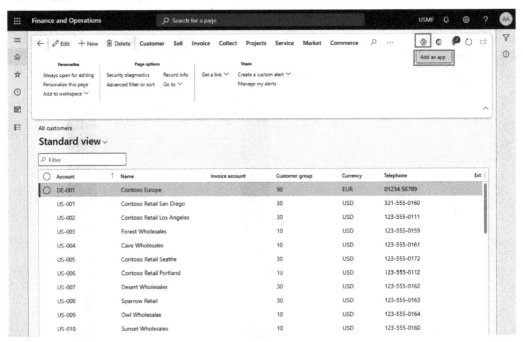

Figure 6.8 – Add an app option in F&O

The **Add an app** button will open a dialog that we will have to complete (see *Figure 6.9*):

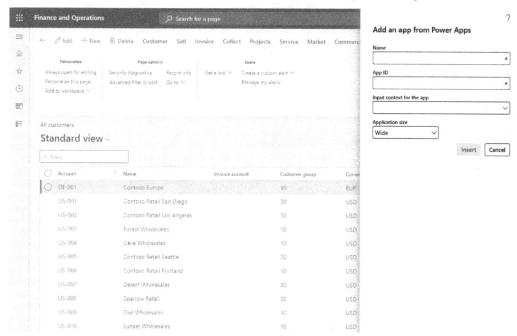

Figure 6.9 – Add an app dialog

We need to complete the values in the dialog to embed the app. The first field, **Name**, is the name we want to give the app in F&O, and it will appear on the list of the Power Apps menu on top of that page.

Then, we need the **App ID** value. We can obtain it from the maker portal in the **Apps** section (see *Figure 6.10*):

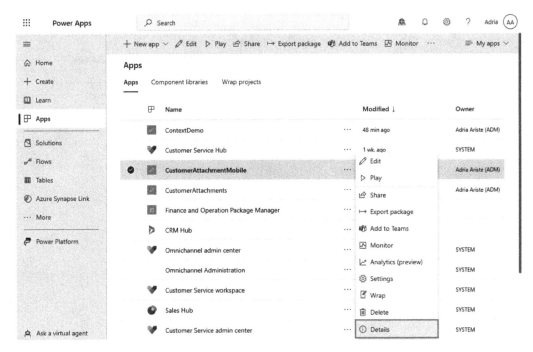

Figure 6.10 – App details

We have to click on the three dots and select **Details**. A new form will open and we will find the App ID there. You can copy its value and use it in the F&O dialog.

Finally, we must select the context (see *Figure 6.11*):

Figure 6.11 – App context

In the case of this app, it'll be the `AccountNum` field of the customer table. Once done, click the **Insert** button. The dialog will close, but if you click again on the Power Apps button, you should see the name you gave the app in the list. Click it and the app will open (see *Figure 6.12*):

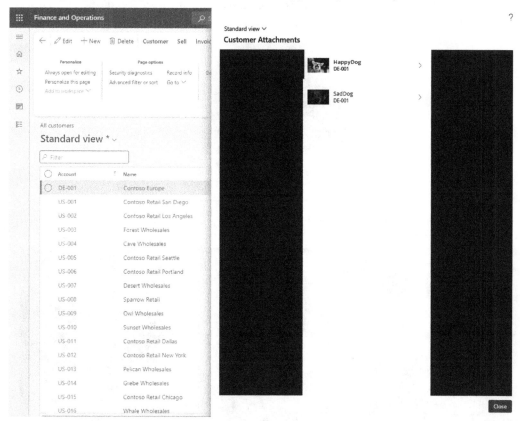

Figure 6.12 – Embedded app in F&O

The app displays two attachments for the customer `DE-001`.

This is one of the methods we can use to embed a Power Apps app in F&O. However, you might be thinking it's not good enough because you're losing access to the F&O side until you close the app. In the next section, we'll learn how we can embed an app using Visual Studio and customizations, and by doing this, we will be able to have a functioning F&O form at the same time as the Power Apps app.

Embed in a form using Visual Studio

Is it possible to avoid the frequent clicking of the Power Apps button on the bar each time we want to open the app? Yes, this can be done by embedding the button using Visual Studio and the Power Apps Host control (see *Figure 6.13*):

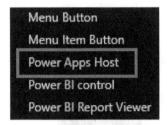

Figure 6.13 – Power Apps Host control

To demonstrate this, I've created a new form on Dynamics 365 F&O to display a list of customers and the Power Apps app (see *Figure 6.14*):

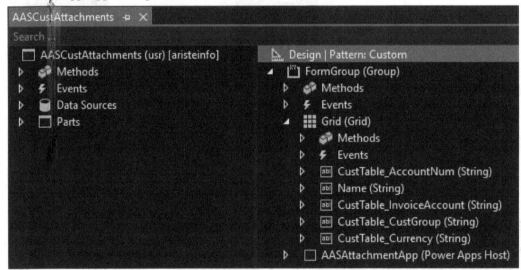

Figure 6.14 – Customer attachments form

This form, as you can see, has a custom pattern featuring just a grid with some fields and the Power Apps Host control.

> **Note**
> All the objects used in this demonstration can be found in the GitHub project for this chapter.

The form displays the grid next to the Power Apps app (see *Figure 6.15*):

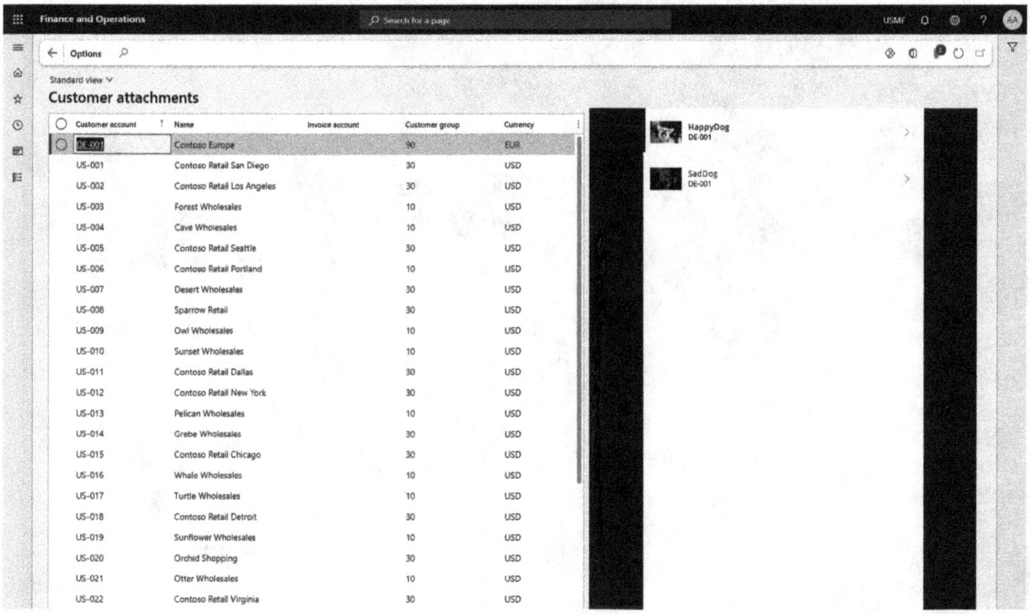

Figure 6.15 – Custom customer attachments form

We can see the list of customers on the left and the Power Apps app loaded on the right. Notice that the F&O grid can be clicked because the app is being displayed inside the F&O form instead of on a modal dialog. Let's see what we need to do in Visual Studio to accomplish this.

Remember what we did when we wanted to embed the app from the UI? We needed a name, the app ID, and the field that we're passing as the context to the Power App. That's exactly what we need to embed it as a customization in Visual Studio, although we don't need the name.

You just need to select the **Power App Control** and go to the **Properties** pane (see *Figure 6.16*):

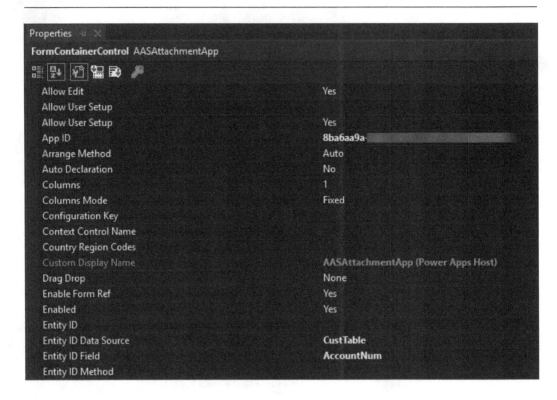

Figure 6.16 – Properties to embed the app in Virtual Studio

We need to fill in the **App ID** property with the same value as we saw in the UI section. The **Entity ID Data Source** will be the table that the field we are using as a context belongs to and **Entity ID Field** is the field from that table.

Once that's configured, our app is ready to be displayed in the form!

Embedding from the dashboard

There's a third way of embedding a Power Apps app in Dynamics 365 F&O. However, it's not meant to use any app context, company, or related table data.

We can create a new tile in the F&O dashboard that will load a full-page Power App. In the dashboard, we need to right-click anywhere, and in the context menu, select the **Personalize** option. A new context menu will open (see *Figure 6.17*):

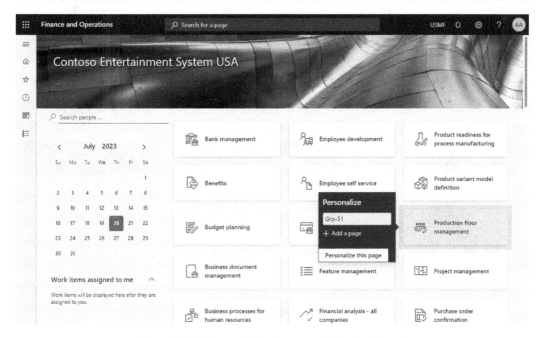

Figure 6.17 – Personalizing the menu in the dashboard

We need to select the + **Add a page** option. A dialog will open, and we need to select the **Power Apps** option. We will see a dialog similar to the one we got when we embedded the app via the UI (see *Figure 6.18*):

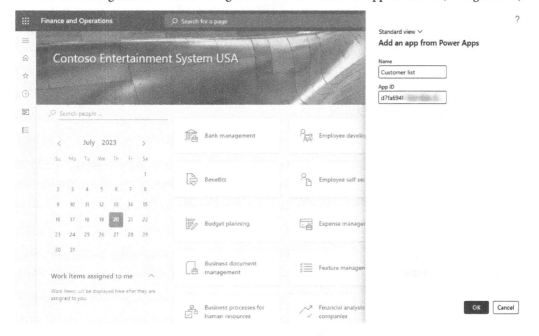

Figure 6.18 – Embedding an app in the dashboard

We will complete both fields:

- The **Name** one will be used as the title of the tile on the dashboard

- The **App ID** field will be the same **App ID** we can find in the maker portal

Click the **OK** button to add it to the dashboard. The tile will appear in the last position. For this example, I've created a tablet Power Apps app (see *Figure 6.19*):

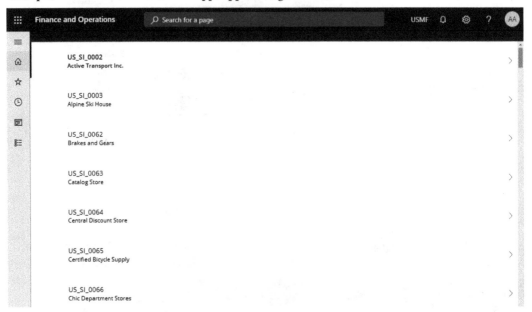

Figure 6.19 – Dashboard Power Apps app

This app is a simple gallery showing a list of customers. We can see that the Power Apps app is displayed in full-screen mode.

> **Note**
> If you need filtering capabilities in a Power Apps app embedded in the dashboard, you will need to build them yourself inside the Power App, as there's no context available. For example, you might add a drop-down menu with the company list that will be used to filter all records by company.

This third way of embedding an app can be useful for F&O users who need to access specific apps. By allowing them to open the Power Apps app from the dashboard, user adoption could be improved.

Summary

In this chapter, we learned how to integrate Power Apps with Dynamics 365 F&O thanks to the context parameters `EntityId` and `Cmp`, creating a link between Power Apps and F&O.

We've also seen how the Power Apps app can be embedded from an F&O form, allowing a seamless and relevant user experience. This feature demonstrates the Power App's ability to accurately reflect active records from F&O.

In subsequent sections, you learned about the various methods of embedding a Power Apps app into F&O. The first is a UI-based approach, presenting the Power Apps app as a modal form, while the second method involves using Visual Studio to incorporate the Power Apps Host control, offering a more integrated user experience. Each method provides different levels of access to F&O while using the app.

The chapter concluded with the exploration of a third embedding method, which included creating a new tile in the F&O dashboard that loads a full-page Power Apps app. However, this method doesn't utilize any app context or related table data from F&O. Instead, we learned how to create a simple customer gallery view using a tablet Power Apps app and to build custom filtering options due to the lack of context availability. By understanding these various techniques, you're equipped to effectively integrate and utilize Power Apps within Dynamics 365 F&O.

In the next chapter, we'll dive into details of how we can build apps in Power Apps using finance and operations data, which connectors to use, and how to trigger OData actions from the app.

Questions

Here are some questions to check your understanding of the chapter. Please see the answers at the end of the chapter.

1. What are the parameters passed in the context of the Power Apps app when embedding it in Dynamics 365 F&O?

    a. `Cmp` and `EntityId`

    b. `AccountNum` and `EntityId`

    c. `EntityId` and `AccountNum`

    d. `Cmp` and `AccountNum`

2. What is the purpose of embedding a Power Apps app in an F&O form?

    a. To display information unrelated to the active record

    b. To show data related to active records from F&O in the app

    c. To allow users to modify the app

    d. To bypass F&O authentication

3. What is the major difference between embedding a Power Apps app into F&O using the UI-based approach and using Visual Studio?

    a. The UI-based approach does not require an App ID

    b. Visual Studio provides a more integrated user experience

    c. The UI-based approach does not need any context from F&O

    d. Visual Studio allows for full-screen app display

4. For the Visual Studio method of embedding a Power App, what properties are necessary?

    a. **Entity ID Field**, **App ID**, and **Entity ID Data Source**

    b. **Name**, **Entity ID Field**, and **Entity ID Data Source**

    c. **App ID** and **Name** only

    d. **Entity ID Field** and **Entity ID Data Source** only

5. When creating a new tile in the F&O dashboard for a full-page Power App, what must you consider?

    a. The app automatically inherits context from the F&O dashboard

    b. You have to manually add filtering capabilities due to the lack of availability of context

    c. The app ID is not necessary

    d. The app will only display data related to the current user

Further reading

To learn more about this chapter, you can refer to the following links:

What is Power Apps?: `https://learn.microsoft.com/en-us/power-apps/powerapps-overview`

Wrap: `https://learn.microsoft.com/en-us/power-apps/maker/common/wrap/overview`

Embed canvas apps from Power Apps: `https://learn.microsoft.com/en-us/dynamics365/fin-ops-core/fin-ops/get-started/embed-power-apps`

Microsoft Power FX overview: `https://learn.microsoft.com/en-us/power-platform/power-fx/overview`

Answers

1. a. `Cmp` and `EntityId`

2. b. To show data related to active records from F&O in the app

3. b. Visual Studio provides a more integrated user experience.

4. a. **Entity ID Field**, **App ID**, and **Entity ID Data Source**

5. b. You have to manually add filtering capabilities due to the lack of availability of context.

7
Extending F&O Apps with Power Apps

Thanks to the integration between Dataverse and F&O environments, we can use F&O virtual tables in Dataverse. This will be the base we will use to create Power Apps to extend the ERP functionality in a list where we can see a list of our customers and where we will update the credit limit from inside the Power App. This will prove how Power Apps can be useful, for example, for a salesperson traveling to customers; instead of accessing the ERP from their mobile phone, they can use a Power App with just the information they need.

In this chapter, we will learn how to display F&O data in a Power App by covering these topics:

- Loading and modifying F&O data into a Power App
- Running `OData` actions from a Power App

Technical requirements

If you have followed the previous chapter, then you've already fulfilled the technical requirements.

The code and project with the objects needed to reproduce the steps in this chapter can be found at `https://github.com/PacktPublishing/Extending-D365-Finance-and-Operation-apps-with-Power-Platform-/tree/main/Chapter%2007`.

Loading and modifying F&O data into a Power App

As we saw when we learned about Power Automate flows, we can use the standard F&O connector or the native Dataverse connector using F&O virtual tables in Dataverse. When working with Power Apps, we can also choose between the standard F&O connector and the native Dataverse connector, if we have virtual tables enabled for our F&O environment.

Once again, using one or the other is a decision you and your team should take before you start building anything. Both connectors will fulfill the requirements and work fine.

In the following sections, we'll learn what's wrong (in my opinion) with the native F&O connector, and why I prefer to use the Dataverse connector. Don't get me wrong, there's nothing wrong with the F&O connector, but Dataverse prefers Dataverse.

Using the F&O standard connector in a canvas app

Let's learn how to create a canvas app using the F&O connector! For this example, we will create a mobile canvas app that will load the customers and show the current credit limit of the customer.

The first step will be going into the maker portal and creating a new canvas app. Select the phone format. After creating it, you should see the designer (see *Figure 7.1*):

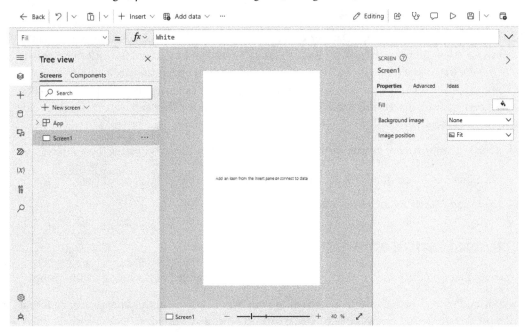

Figure 7.1 – Overview of a canvas app's designer

As we learned in the previous chapter, the designer is comprised of a center block with the app view and a left pane with several options such as the tree view, data, variables, and Power Automate flows that the app has. In the right pane, we can see the properties of the currently selected element.

Now, we will add the connection to our F&O environment. Click on the data menu from the right pane – the one that has a classic database icon. This will change the content of the right pane and you will see an **Add data** button. Click it and a dialog will open (see *Figure 7.2*):

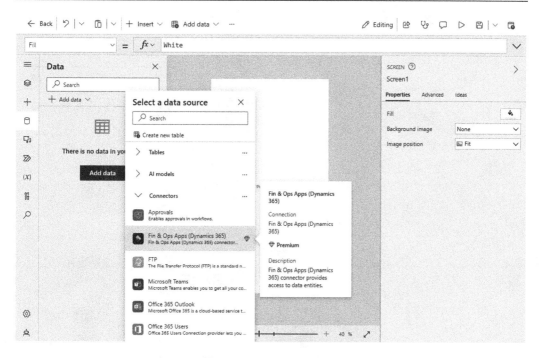

Figure 7.2 – Adding a data connection to the Power App

You will see three sections in the dialog:

- **Tables**: These are the tables that exist in the current Dataverse environment in which you're creating the app

- **AI models**: AI builder models in the current Dataverse environment

- **Connectors**: Like in Power Automate, these are connectors that connect to Microsoft and third-party services connectors

> **Licenses**
>
> If the F&O connector does not appear in the list, make sure your tenant has available F&O licenses.

Open the **Connectors** section; you'll see the **Fin & Ops Apps (Dynamics 365)** connector. Click it twice – once to select it and a second time to open the **Choose a dataset** pane (see *Figure 7.3*):

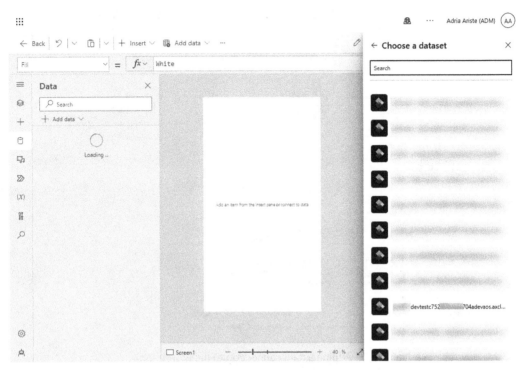

Figure 7.3 – Environment selection in F&O the connector

This will display all the environments to which your user has access. Select the right one and the list of public data entities in F&O will be shown. For our example, we'll use the **CustomersV3** entity. Once you've selected it, the connector will be displayed in the right pane, under the **Data** menu.

> **Don't mix environments!**
>
> You might be tempted to use the same Dataverse environment to create Power Apps that use connectors to different F&O environments. While there's nothing wrong with that, I'd recommend not doing it. It's only a matter of how you organize yourself and your projects, but I think it's better to only work with the F&O environment that is linked to the Dataverse one.
>
> However, the F&O connector doesn't need your F&O and Dataverse environments to be linked, and this recommendation would be not applicable. Just keep in mind that you need to be organized and not mix connectors to several environments in the same app.

The next step will be adding a vertical gallery to our app. Vertical galleries are components that allow us to display a list of records from our connector nicely, with some out-of-the-box pre-defined templates and customizable fields, as well as images.

Click on the **Insert** option in the top menu bar and select the **Vertical gallery** component. It will show you the pre-defined view with some lorem ipsum placeholders. Change your right pane to the tree view and click the **Gallery** component. A dialog will open in the **GALLERY** area and show the connector we configured earlier.

> **Note**
>
> For this example, make sure that the user that you're using to create and access the Power App exists in the F&O environment you'll be targeting, and also that its default company is not DAT. You can change your user's default company in the user information form inside F&O.

Click it and you'll see the contents of the gallery being updated. With the **Gallery1** component selected, go to the **Property** pane and under **Layout**, select the **Title, subtitle, and body** layout (see *Figure 7.4*):

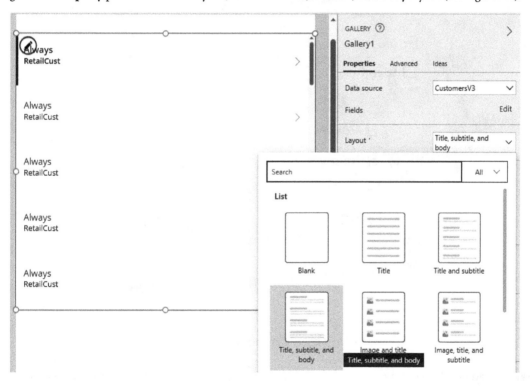

Figure 7.4 – Gallery layouts

There are several available. When you select one of the layouts, the components of the gallery will be updated. For example, if you change it to a layout that has an image, it will automatically add the image component to the **GALLERY** area. You can see which components exist in the **GALLERY** area by clicking the > button next to the name on the tree view while working inside the tree view (see *Figure 7.5*):

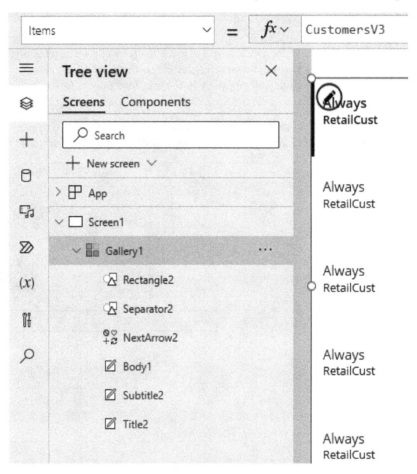

Figure 7.5 – Gallery component components

With the layout we've selected, we can see the gallery component is comprised of the following components:

- Two shapes: **Rectangle2** and **Separator2**
- An image: **NextArrow2**
- Three labels: **Body1**, **Subtitle2**, and **Title2**

We can select each component of the gallery and change their properties or rename them. Speaking about renaming things, this is also an internal decision on how you want to name things, but there's a best practice developers follow that involves giving variables a name that describes what they're used for. For non-technical users, this would be the same – for example, naming Word files with a short description of the content of the document so that you know what's in the file.

We should be doing the same with the components of a Power App. Now, I'm going to rename the components in my app; they'll look like this (see *Figure 7.6*):

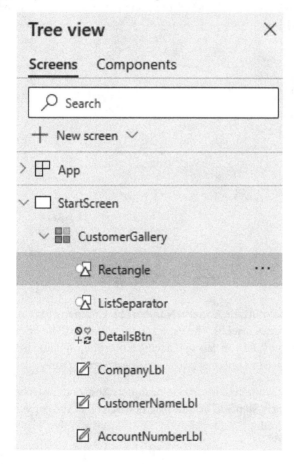

Figure 7.6 – Renamed components

I've renamed the screen `StartScreen` as this will be the initial screen that will load when the app opens. I've changed the labels to a description + Lbl pattern so that I know those are labels and what they contain. I've also renamed the arrow image to `DetailsBtn` because although it's not a button, it will behave like one.

> **Naming elements**
>
> As I mentioned previously, naming is something that you need to decide within your team. You could skip doing it, but believe me that when you start building more complex apps, and you end up with a screen that has `Label1`, `Label2`, `Label3`, and up to as many labels as you have, it will be harder to know what each label is used for.

The next thing we will do is change which information the gallery is showing. Select the gallery in the tree view and from the right pane, click the **Edit** button next to the **Fields** property. This will open a new pane (see *Figure 7.7*):

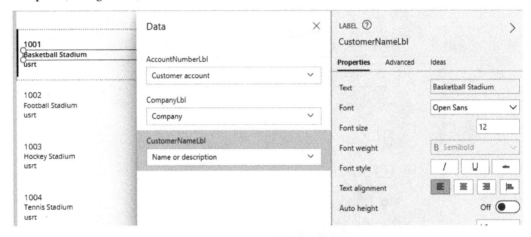

Figure 7.7 – Gallery fields

We will select **Customer account** for **AccountNumberLbl**, **Company** for **CompanyLbl**, and **Name or description** for **CustomerNameLbl**. The values in the gallery will be updated when you change which field is being displayed. As you can see, having a meaningful name for each component also helps us identify what we need to select as the label values! Naming things properly is important.

Now, we'll see a screen that contains a list of our customers, showing the customer account number, name, and company. The next step will be adding a new screen to the app where the credit limit of the customer will be displayed.

We can do that by going to the tree view and clicking the **New screen** button. Click the blank layout and a new screen component called **Screen2** will be added to the left pane. Rename it `CreditLimitScreen`.

For this one, we will add the components ourselves. We'll add four label components; we will use two of them as pure labels that display `Customer:` and `Credit limit:`; the other two will display the values dynamically and change depending on the customer we select. Remember to give meaningful names to these labels. I'm insisting on this a lot, but I guarantee it will make your life easier.

How will we display the value on the labels? We will be using variables. From the tree view, select the **App** component and, in the property selector, select **OnStart** (see *Figure 7.8*):

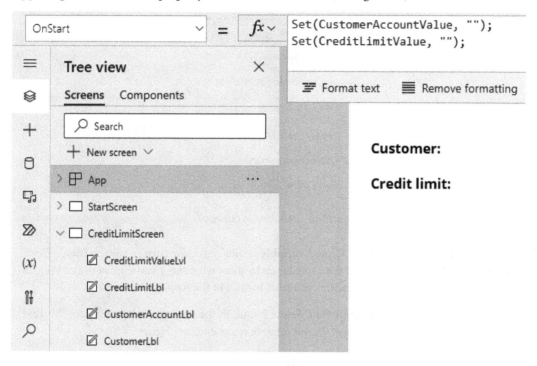

Figure 7.8 – Declaring variables

Here, we'll declare our variables using the **Set** function and the following formulas:

```
Set(CustomerAccountValue, "");
```

```
Set(CreditLimitValue, "");
```

Doing this will initialize two global variables named *CustomerAccountValue* and *CreditLimitValue* with an empty value when the app starts. When we declare variables, we can see them and track their values via the **Variables** section on the left pane (see *Figure 7.9*):

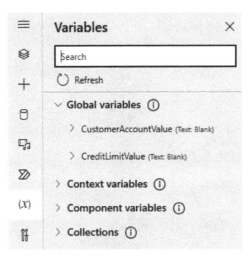

Figure 7.9 – Variables in our app

We can see both variables under the **Global variables** node, and their current values, **Blank**. Once we have the variables ready, we want the value labels to show what these variables contain. We will also use the Set formula but this time on each label instead of the **App** node.

First, we'll consider **CustomerAccountLbl**. Select it and, in the property selector, select the **Text** property. There, we will use the value of the variable we've created (see *Figure 7.10*):

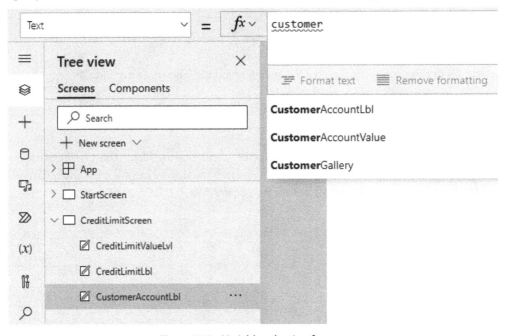

Figure 7.10 – Variable selection for text

When we start typing on the formula bar, we will get some help. If we start typing customer, it will show the **CustomerAccountValue** variable there; select it. The text of the label will disappear as the current value of the variable is empty. Do the same for the credit limit value label.

What we want to accomplish now is that when the user presses the arrow button on the **StartScreen** screen, **CreditScreen** appears, and the right values are displayed. Let's do that!

Go back to **StartScreen** and select the **DetailsBtn** component, select the **OnSelect** property, and use the Navigate function, like this:

```
Navigate(CreditLimitScreen)
```

Here, CreditLimitScreen is the name of the second screen; change it if you've named it differently. The Navigate function is used to change the current screen. We need to do the same on the credit limit screen (see *Figure 7.11*):

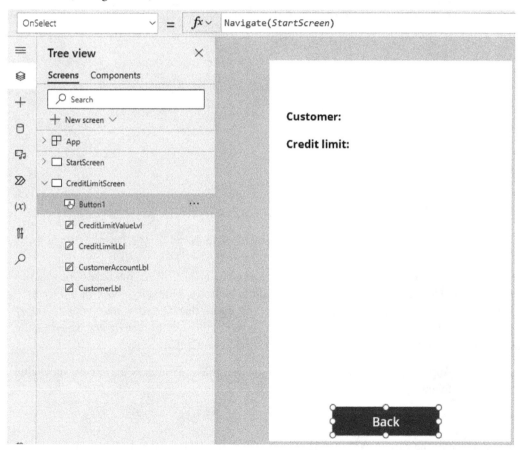

Figure 7.11 – The Back button

I've used a button component that has the `Navigate` function in the **OnSelect** property, pointing to the starting screen. You could also use a shape, such as a back arrow. The design is up to you!

We can go from one screen to the other – we're just missing the aspect of loading the right values when we navigate to the credit limit details screen, but that will be very easy to do. Select the **CreditLimitScreen** screen on the tree view and use the following formulas:

```
Set(CustomerAccountValue, CustomerGallery.Selected.'Customer
account');
Set(CreditLimitValue, CustomerGallery.Selected.'Credit limit');
```

In this formula, we're getting the selected item of the gallery component (with the **CustomerGallery. Selected** part of the formula) and selecting **Customer account** for the **CustomerAccountValue** variable and **Credit limit** for the **CreditLimitValue** variable.

And… is that all? I've you've been following along, you should see an error in your app (see *Figure 7.12*):

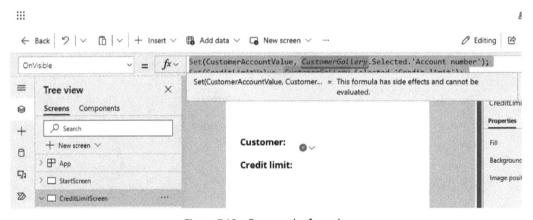

Figure 7.12 – Error on the formula

See the red cross icon on **CreditLimitValueLbl**? What is going on here? If you're a developer, you may already have an idea of the issue. When we declared the variables, I initialized both with the empty string value (`" "`). Variables in Power Apps are typed. This means that if I declare them with the empty string value, the Power App will always expect a string to be stored in those variables. Note that the credit limit field is returning a numeric value, not a string. Let's fix that.

Go back to the **App** component in the tree view and change the `Set` formula of the **CreditLimitValue** variable to the following:

```
Set(CreditLimitValue, 0);
```

This will initialize the variable with a number type. If we go to the **CreditLimitScreen** screen, the error will be gone. Now, if we run the app and click the arrow button next to a customer row, we will see its credit limit value (see *Figure 7.13*):

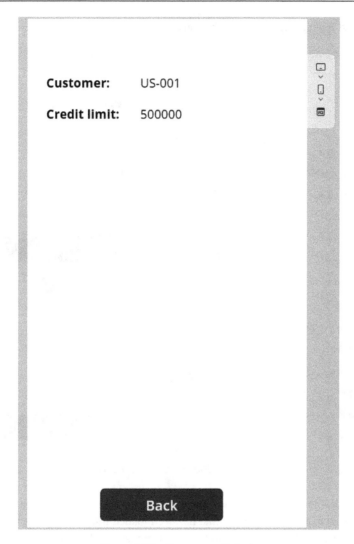

Figure 7.13 – Current credit limit

With that, we've learned how to display Dynamics 365 F&O data in a canvas app using the standard connector, and we've seen it's quite easy. Now, let's learn how we can update it.

Updating data using the F&O connector

The example we've just seen is nice if we just need to display data. But what if we also need to update some of it? I will show you this using the same Power App.

Here, I've added a text input component and a button to the **CreditLimitScreen** screen (see *Figure 7.14*):

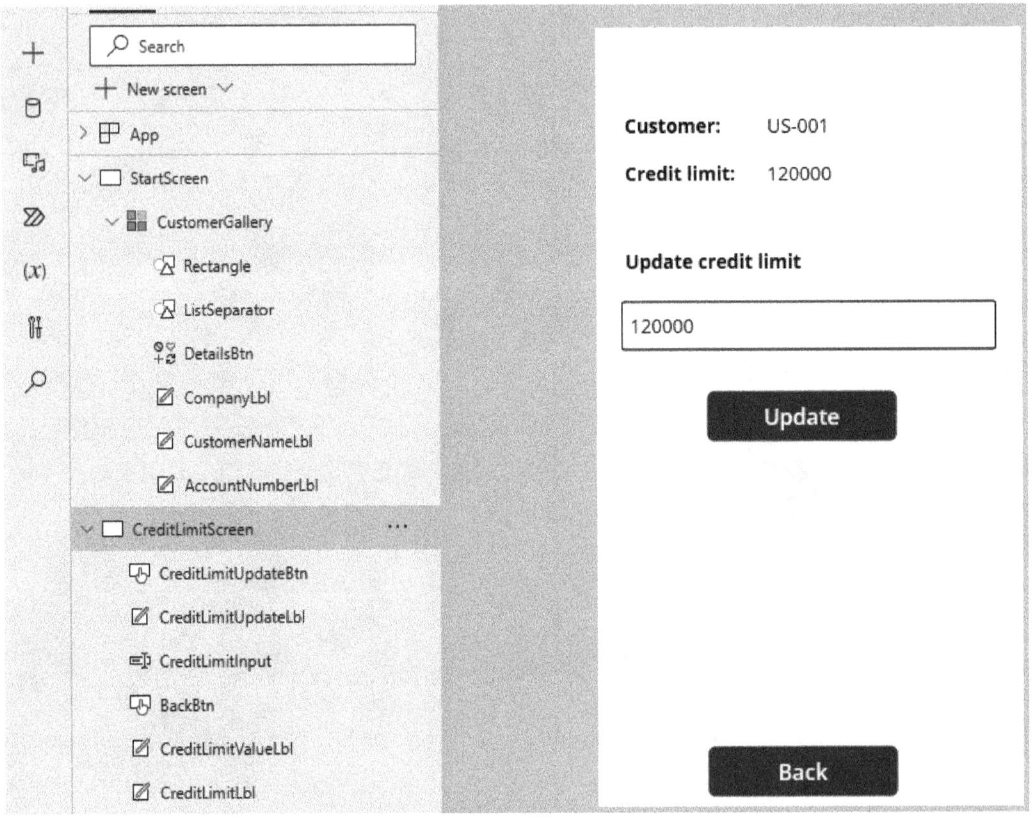

Figure 7.14 – The Update button for F&O data

When the screen loads, the text input field will display the same value as the current credit limit. Text input controls allow us to change the value that has been loaded into the control. But changing the value in the text input control isn't enough to trigger the update, and that's why we need the button to call the Patch function. In the OnSelected property of the button, we will do this:

```
Patch(
    'CustomersV3',
    LookUp('CustomersV3', 'Customer account' = CustomerGallery.
Selected.'Customer account'),
    {
        'Credit limit': Value(CreditLimitInput.Text)
    }
);
Refresh(CustomersV3);
Set(CreditLimitValue, Value(CreditLimitInput.Text));
```

We must pass the Patch function three parameters: the data source we want to update, the record that we will update, and the new value we want it to have. In our case, the data source is the CustomersV3 entity.

The record to be updated is selected using the LookUp function, which needs two parameters: the data source where it has to find the single record (the one we will update using the Patch function), and the search condition, which uses the currently selected record in the gallery as a filter.

The new value that the credit limit value will have is updated using the JSON string that sets the credit limit field equal to what we have in the text input control. Beware because the text input will return a string, and the credit limit field is expecting a number; that's why we use the Value function – to cast the string into a number.

In the last two lines, we will refresh the data source so that when it's reloaded, we'll see the new values, and we'll be able to assign the new credit limit to the label.

If you try this, you will see that it takes a while. This is one of the reasons I prefer the Dataverse connector over the F&O one.

And there's another reason too. If you go to **StartScreen**, you will notice that all users shown are from the same company. Which company? The one that the user accessing the Power App has as the default in the **UserInfo** screen in F&O. This means that the standard F&O connector will only show the records from a single company.

If this limitation isn't a blocker, you could perfectly use the F&O connector. Once again, this is something that needs to be defined in the analysis and design phases.

Using F&O virtual tables in a canvas app

Now that we know about the F&O connector, we're going to create the canvas app using the F&O virtual tables in Dataverse. This will make use of the tables in the current environment, meaning we must have enabled them and activated the **CustomersV3** virtual table to do this.

So, let's start by connecting the app to the **CustomersV3** virtual table. Unlike what we did in the previous section, we don't need to configure any connector. Just add a new vertical gallery and configure the data source (see *Figure 7.15*):

Figure 7.15 – Configuring the virtual table as a data source

In this case, we can use the top filter and search for `mserp`. We talked about this when we learned about virtual tables: the F&O virtual tables in Dataverse have this suffix in the name and we can use it to look for them. For this example, it will be the **CustomersV3** one.

Change the layout, as we did before, to show the customer account number, name, and company of each record. Now, before continuing, preview or run the app. Notice something? It's already showing data from all companies. That's the first advantage of using the native Dataverse connector.

We will do one thing now, and that is to add a drop-down control that will allow us to filter the records that are being displayed in the gallery. To do this, we need an additional virtual table: the company's one, named **CompanyInfoEntity**.

Once you've enabled it on Dataverse, go back to the app and add a label and a drop-down control on top (see *Figure 7.16*):

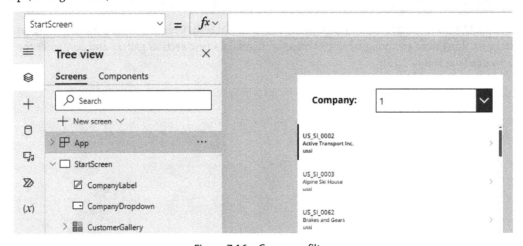

Figure 7.16 – Company filter

Place them on top and set the label value to Companies:. The next step will be displaying the values in the dropdown. Select the drop-down control and click on the **Items** property (see *Figure 7.17*):

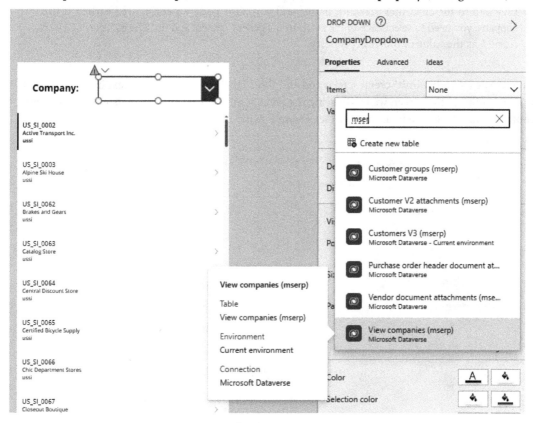

Figure 7.17 – Adding company data to the dropdown

Once more, use the mserp filter and look for the **View companies** virtual table. This will add it as a data source to the app. Make sure that the **Value** property is set to **DataArea**. Now, we have all the companies from our F&O instance in the dropdown. The next step is using the selected value to filter the visible items in the gallery.

To do that, select the gallery control, then go to the **Items** property in the property selector and use this formula:

```
Filter('Customers V3 (mserp)', 'Company Code' = CompanyDropdown.
Selected.DataArea)
```

The Filter function is used to filter records in a dataset. In our case, we're filtering the Customers V3 table, where the company code is equal to the selected company in the drop-down control.

> **Note**
>
> It is possible that after changing the **Items** property in the gallery, the controls lose the binding they had to the customer account, name, and company code we configured earlier. If this happens, you need to select each of the labels in the gallery control and use `ThisItem.'Field name'` as the value of the **Text** property.

Now, create a **CreditLimitScreen** screen and add three label controls and one text input control. It will be similar to the screen we made using the F&O control except that we're using the text input control to update the credit limit value (see *Figure 7.18*):

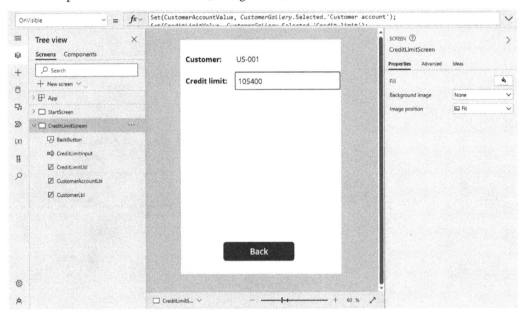

Figure 7.18 – Details screen with text input

Remember to declare the variables as we did for the F&O connector, and then use them to set the values of the customer account label and credit limit input text. Also, add the **Back** button, which will return the user to the previous screen.

Now, instead of using a button to update the record, we will update the field when the value is changed. Select the text input and in its `OnChange` property, set this formula:

```
Patch('Customers V3 (mserp)',
    LookUp('Customers V3 (mserp)', 'Customer account' =
CustomerGallery.Selected.'Customer account'),
    {
        'Credit limit': Value(CreditLimitInput.Text)
```

```
    }
);
Refresh('Customers V3 (mserp)');
```

You can see it's the same as the one we used for the **Update** button in the F&O connector section. When we exit the input control, it triggers the `Patch` function. Now, we're ready to test our app. I have selected the **US-003** customer (see *Figure 7.19*):

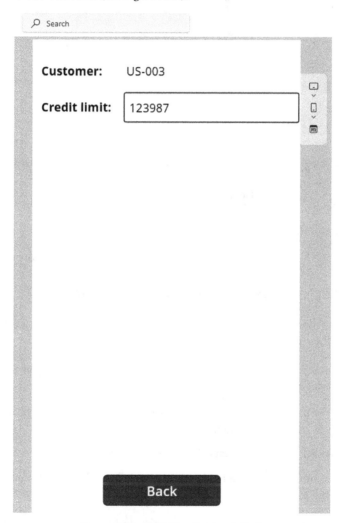

Figure 7.19 – Updating the credit limit

I have set the new credit limit value to 123987. If I go to F&O, I will see it's been updated (see *Figure 7.20*):

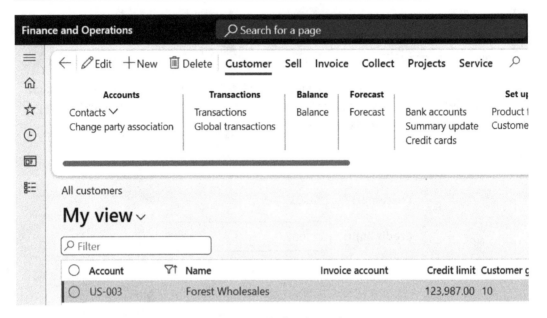

Figure 7.20 – Updated record

US-003 has had its credit limit value updated to `123987`.

In this scenario, the `Patch` function is faster thanks to using the Dataverse connector.

The F&O connector versus the Dataverse connector

With that, we've learned how to use the F&O connector and the Dataverse connector using F&) virtual tables. In both cases, the app is very similar, but we have some conclusions:

- The F&O connector always shows the records from the default company of the user who's opening the Power App

- The Dataverse connector shows data from all the companies, and we may filter the items in the gallery if we want to see some of them

- The `Patch` operation is faster when using the Dataverse connector

- Using the F&O connector, we can load data from a different F&O environment, not only the one linked to the Dataverse one

So, when should we use one or the other? Once again, it's a design decision. Let me insist on this: the F&O connector is perfectly fine if you want to use it.

You may have a Dataverse environment that's on a different tenant than your F&O instances. In that case, the F&O connector will be useful and probably your only option.

In the future, thanks to the **One Dynamics One Platform** program that's bringing the ERP and Dataverse closer to working as a single platform, it will be more unusual to have separate or unlinked environments. In that case, using the Dataverse connector could be an easy decision.

And of course, we can't forget licensing. F&O licensing allows licensed users to create and use Power Apps that use F&O data at no additional cost. But if you use virtual tables and the users accessing those apps have only a Power App license, they will need an F&O license too. Planning this is important.

Running OData actions from a Power App

We've seen how to display and update data from F&O into a Power App, but what can we do if we want to trigger some process on the F&O side from the Power App? Well, thankfully, we have OData actions in F&O data entities! And we can call them from a Power App thanks to Power Automate!

Imagine a scenario where we have a Power App for a salesperson, and this app shows a list of sales orders. The salesperson wants to be able to post a sales order invoice from the app. We just need to create an OData action in the **Sales Orders** entity that does this. Let's learn how!

> **Extending data entities**
>
> Unfortunately, it's not possible to create code extensions for data entities. This forces us to duplicate data entities if we want to change code or add methods.

To do this, we will need to do some X++ development work in Visual Studio. Duplicate the standard `SalesOrderHeadersV2` entity and add a new method, like this:

```
[SysODataAction('AASPostSalesOrder', false)]
    public static str postSalesorder(SalesId _salesId)
    {
        SalesFormLetter salesFormLetter;
        salesTable salesTable;

        salesTable = SalesTable::find(_salesId);
        salesFormLetter = SalesFormLetter::construct(DocumentSta-
tus::Invoice);

        salesFormLetter.update(salesTable, DateTimeUtil::date(Date-
TimeUtil::applyTimeZoneOffset(DateTimeUtil::utcNow(), DateTimeU-
til::getCompanyTimeZone())), SalesUpdate::All, AccountOrder::None,
NoYes::No, NoYes::Yes);

        return CustInvoiceJour::findRecId(salesFormLetter.parmJournal-
Record().RecId).InvoiceId;
    }
```

Notice the `SysODataAction` attribute on top of the method? This is what defines this method as an `OData` action. We will be able to use it from a Power Automate flow that will expect one parameter: the `SalesId` parameter of the sales order we want to post.

> **Duplicate data entities**
>
> When duplicating a data entity from the standard, remember that you must change its label, public name, and collection name so that it can be built and synchronized. For example, you can add your own prefix to them. This would make **CustomersV3 AASCustomersV3** if I used my AAS prefix for it. The same goes for the label, from **Customers (V3)** to **Customers AAS**, for example.

Go back to the maker portal and create a new phone canvas app. This app will have a gallery showing the sales orders and a button (see *Figure 7.21*):

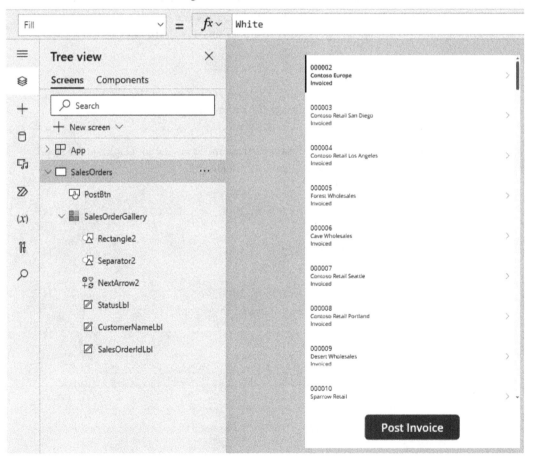

Figure 7.21 – Sales orders app

The **Post Invoice** button will be used to post the invoice of the selected sales order, if open. And we need a Power Automate flow to do that! Go to the right menu bar and select **Power Automate**, then click the **Create new flow** button and finally the **Create from blank** button. The flow designer will open.

This will be an instant cloud flow whose trigger will be the Power Apps one. Now, add an action of the **Execute action** type (see *Figure 7.22*):

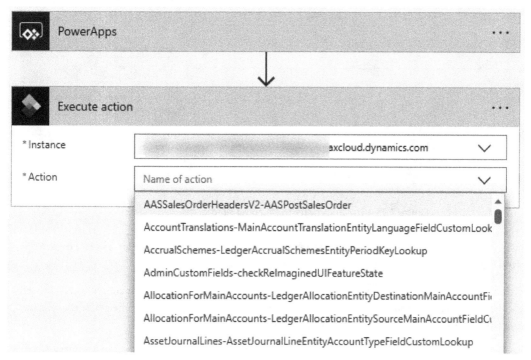

Figure 7.22 – Executing the OData action from the flow

Select your environment and then, in the action list, look for the one we've created. Mine is the first one thanks to its name. The action block will refresh and show a `_salesId` field (see *Figure 7.23*):

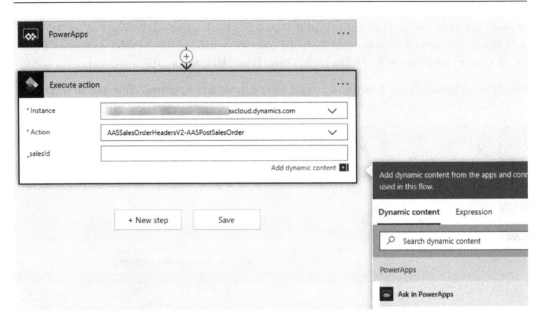

Figure 7.23 – The parameter to be completed in the Power App

Click inside to complete it. At this point, the **Dynamic content** dialog will show an **Ask in PowerApps** option. Select it and save the flow.

Go back to the maker portal; you should see your new flow on the **Power Automate** section in the left pane. Now, we can use it in the button of our app. Just select the button and in the property selector, choose the OnSelect property and add the following formula:

```
PostSalesOrder.Run(SalesOrderGallery.Selected.'Sales order')
```

PostSalesOrder is the name that you have given to your flow, so if you've named it differently, you need to change that. The .Run part calls the execution of the flow. The parameter inside the brackets is the expected value of the SalesId parameter that the method in the data entity we created earlier is expecting. The value of this parameter is the sales order number of the selected element in the gallery.

Let's create a sales order in F&O. I'm using a Contoso demo database. In the company's USMF, I will create a sales order with the **US-001** customer, and in that order a single line for item number 1000 (see *Figure 7.24*):

Sales order lines

		CW quantity	CW unit	Quantity	Unit	Delivery type		CW deliver...	Adjusted u...	Site		Warehouse	Unit pric
○	⟳												
●				1.00	ea	Stock			0.00000	1		13	1,900.000

Figure 7.24 – Open sales order

You can use any data, just make sure there's an available quantity of the item you will use and that the customer is not on hold. You can see that the sales order I've created is open. Now, in the Power App, look for that order (see *Figure 7.25*):

Figure 7.25 – Posting the order from the Power App

We will see that the order is open too, so just select the row and click the **Post Invoice** button. This will trigger the Power Automate flow (see *Figure 7.26*):

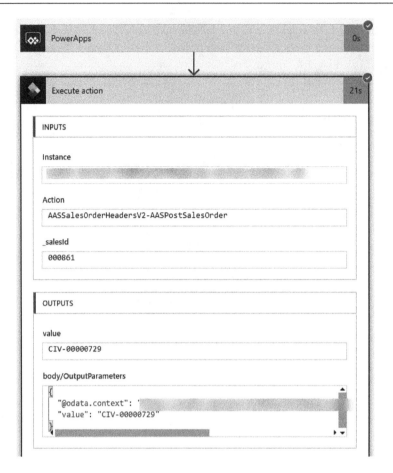

Figure 7.26 – Flow run

Here, we can see the name of the `OData` action (`AASSalesOrderHeadersV2-AASPostSalesOrder`) and the sales order number (`000861`). The action has finished successfully; if we go to the sales orders form in F&O, we will be able to see this (see *Figure 7.27*):

Figure 7.27 – Posted sales order

The sales order has been successfully posted from the Power App thanks to a Power Automate flow and the `OData` action that we have created!

In the next chapter, we'll learn how we can integrate a data lake so that we can extract data from F&O and use it in Power BI reports!

Summary

In this chapter, we learned how the integration between Dataverse and F&O environments has opened new opportunities for app development thanks to Power Apps. This integration allows users to use F&O Virtual tables in Dataverse as a foundation to create Power Apps that improve and extend the ERP functionality.

There are two main connectors to consider: the standard F&O connector and the Dataverse connector. While the F&O connector is limited to displaying records from the default company of the user accessing the Power App, the Dataverse connector can display data from all companies. The Dataverse connector also allows faster `Patch` operations. However, the choice between the two often comes down to specific project requirements, licensing considerations, and whether the F&O and Dataverse environments are linked.

A practical application of this integration is, for example, creating a sales order app. Through the use of `OData` actions in F&O data entities, processes in F&O can be triggered directly from the Power App. For instance, a salesperson can post a sales order invoice directly from the app. This integration demonstrates the potential of combining F&O with Power Apps to streamline and enhance business processes.

Questions

Answer the following questions to test your knowledge of this chapter:

1. What is the primary benefit of integrating Dataverse and F&O environments?

    a. It allows for better graphics in Power Apps

    b. It enables the use of F&O Virtual tables in Dataverse

    c. It increases the security of the ERP system

    d. It reduces the cost of Power Apps

2. Which connector displays records only from the default company of the user accessing the Power App?

    a. Dataverse connector

    b. F&O connector

    c. `OData` connector

    d. Power Automate connector

3. What function is used to change the current screen in a Power App?

   a. `Change()`

   b. `Move()`

   c. `Navigate()`

   d. `Switch()`

4. Why might someone choose the Dataverse connector over the F&O connector?

   a. It only shows data from one company

   b. It has slower `Patch` operations

   c. It displays data from all companies

   d. It requires additional licensing

5. In the practical application described, what action can a salesperson perform directly from the Power App?

   a. Create a new customer profile

   b. Delete a sales order

   c. Post a sales order invoice

   d. Adjust the inventory levels

Further reading

To learn more about the topics that were covered in this chapter, take a look at the following resources:

Fin & Ops Apps (Dynamics 365) connector: `https://learn.microsoft.com/en-us/connectors/dynamicsax/`

Patch function in Power Apps: `https://learn.microsoft.com/en-us/power-platform/power-fx/reference/function-patch`

Back and Navigate functions in Power Apps: `https://learn.microsoft.com/en-us/power-platform/power-fx/reference/function-navigate`

Gallery control in Power Apps: `https://learn.microsoft.com/en-us/power-apps/maker/canvas-apps/controls/control-gallery`

Understanding variables in canvas apps: `https://learn.microsoft.com/en-us/power-apps/maker/canvas-apps/working-with-variables`

Use the Power Automate pane: `https://learn.microsoft.com/en-us/power-apps/maker/canvas-apps/working-with-flows`

Power Automate and MSDyn365FO deep dive series: `https://jatomas.com/en/2020/11/30/power-automate-msdyn365fo-deep-dive-i/`

Answers

Here are the answers to this chapter's questions:

1. b. It enables the use of F&O Virtual tables in Dataverse
2. b. F&O connector
3. c. `Navigate()`
4. c. It displays data from all companies
5. c. Post a sales order invoice

8

Power BI Reporting for Dynamics 365 F&O Apps

In Dynamics 365 **Finance & Operations** (**F&O**), we can use the workspaces with embedded Power BI dashboards. These reports use **Entity Store**, and in this chapter, we'll learn how we use **Azure Data Lake Storage** as a source to create Power BI reports.

We won't be using the **Bring Your Own Database** (**BYOD**) method to extract data from Dynamics 365 F&O. It's still possible to use it, but it's more limited than using the newer Synapse Link feature because it can also export tables and not only data entities.

With the features described in this chapter, we will be able to export data from Dynamics 365 F&O into an **Azure Data Lake Storage** account and use it later from Power BI or other BI tools.

Now, let's look into the following:

- The **Entity Store** and embedded Power BI
- Exporting to Data Lake and Synapse Link

Technical requirements

If you followed the previous chapters, you already have the technical prerequisites that are needed for this chapter.

However, if you want to follow the *Exporting to Data Lake and Synapse Link* section, you will also need an Azure subscription whereby you can deploy resources such as storage accounts or key vaults, and create application registrations in Microsoft Entra ID (previously known as Azure Active Directory).

The Entity Store and embedded Power BI

We will start this chapter by talking about the **Entity Store** and seeing why it's useful but also limited if we want to create new reports.

The **Entity Store** is a built-in data store in Dynamics 365 F&O. If you've ever opened **SQL Server Management Studio** (**SSMS**) in a development VM, you'll have probably seen a database called AxDW; this is where **Entity Store** data resides.

And what is using this data? If you're familiar with F&O workspaces, you have probably seen some dashboards being displayed there. These dashboards are Power BI reports that are displayed inside F&O and that consume the data in the **Entity Store** (see *Figure 8.1*):

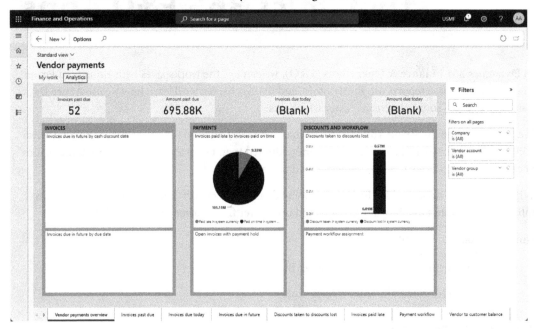

Figure 8.1 – Vendor payments workspace

For example, in the **Vendor payments** workspace, we see the **Analytics** tab. This tab contains a Power BI report that's loading data from the **Entity Store**. These are known as analytical workspaces.

However, this may not be working as expected after deploying a Dynamics 365 F&O environment. Let's learn how to configure it and refresh data.

Refreshing the Entity Store

You need to take this action if you access any dashboards containing an embedded Power BI report and see error messages (see *Figure 8.2*):

Figure 8.2 – Error messages on the Financial analysis workspace

Usually, errors such as the ones shown in *Figure 8.2* will be one or more (or even all) Power BI components embedded in the workspace displaying the message `Can't display the visual` and an infolog error that reads `QueryUserError`.

This means that the **Entity Store** data needs to be refreshed. First of all, go to the **Batch job** page, in `System administration > Inquiries > Batch jobs`.

There, look for the following batch jobs:

- **Deploy measurement**
- **Full reset**
- **Incremental update**

Delete the ones that are in a **Waiting** status and go to **System administration** > **Setup** > **Entity store** (see *Figure 8.3*):

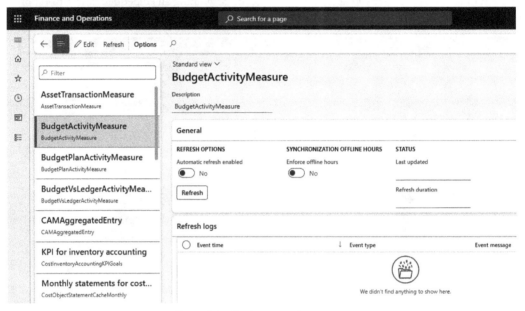

Figure 8.3 – Entity store setup menu

This form shows all the available measures in the **Entity Store** and allows us to refresh them manually with the **Refresh** button. It's also possible to schedule an automated refresh (see *Figure 8.4*):

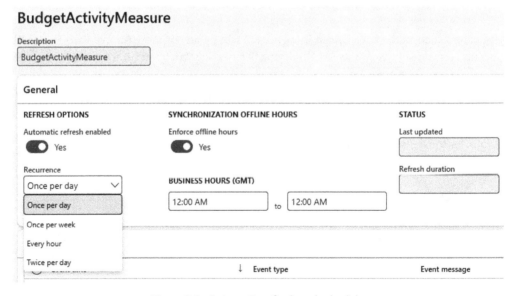

Figure 8.4 – Automatic refresh and schedule

If we want to enable more than one entity, we must do it for each entity individually, and we can choose between the following refresh frequencies:

- **Once per day**

- **Once per week**

- **Every hour**

- **Twice a day**

We can also specify during which hours the refresh can't be done with the **Enforce offline hours** checkbox.

Now, how do we know which entities we want to refresh or configure for automated refresh? If we go to the workspace where we see the error and click on the **See details** link, we will see the following dialog (see *Figure 8.5*):

Couldn't load the data for this visual   ×

Expression.Error: The key didn't match any rows in the table.. Key = [ccon][Schema = "dbo", Item = "LedgerCovLiquidityMeasurement_LedgerCovLiquidityInflowOutflowBalanceEnterprise"]. Table = #table({"Name", "Data", "Schema", "Item", "Kind"}, {}). [/ccon];The key didn't match any rows in the table.. The exception was raised by the IDbCommand interface.

Please try again later or contact support. If you contact support, please provide these details.

See details ˅

Contact support   Close

Figure 8.5 – Error message details in analytical workspace

In the message, look for `Item`; after that, you will see the name of the measure that needs to be refreshed. In this case, it's `LedgerCovLiquidityMeasurement_ LedgerCovLiquidityInflowOutflowBalanceEnterprise`, so the measure we need to refresh is the `LedgerCovLiquidityMeasurement` one.

> **Power BI measures**
>
> A measure is a key concept used in data modeling to perform calculations on data in your model. In Power BI, it is a formula created for data analysis and is used in reporting.

Go back to the **Entity Store** setup form and look for it. Then, either click the **Refresh** button or enable the **Automatic refresh enabled** checkbox and set a frequency. This will create the needed batch jobs again, and once they run, our issue will be solved (see *Figure 8.6*):

Figure 8.6 – Financial insights workspace fixed

The section of the report that was previously displaying the error is now showing the right data in the **Cash flow** piece of the report.

Why is the Entity Store not enough?

The **Entity Store** is a nice out-of-the-box feature that we will definitely use and that helps display data in a very visual manner in the default workspaces. But what if we want to create new reports?

We can use the **Entity Store** of course, have a developer create new measures in Visual Studio, and enable the PowerBI.com integration to deploy the new reports and measures.

But I wouldn't recommend that. Why? It's a totally fine approach if you choose to go with it. I've said this previously: most of the decisions you take need to go with a previous analysis, and if during that analysis you decide that the path you're going with is the right one for your business scenario, go with it.

Instead, when you need to create a Power BI report, go with one of the options in the next sections of this chapter that covers Azure Data Lake integration or Synapse Link. We will look into why I believe those are better options than the **Entity Store** in the next parts of the chapter.

Exporting to Data Lake and Synapse Link

The first alternative to the **Entity Store** is exporting the data to an **Azure Data Lake**, then processing the unstructured data from the lake and having it available in a Synapse workspace. This was a long-awaited feature for Dynamics 365 F&O because in previous versions of Dynamics AX, we, as end users or partners, usually had ownership of the infrastructure where the database was. This meant that we could access the production database to create a read-only copy that was used for reporting.

When the cloud version of Dynamics AX 7 (the first name F&O had) was released, that option was not there, and we lost a method that was used by a lot of people to extract data and create reports. And even for a short period of time, we didn't even have the BYOD functionality.

> **What about BYOD?**
>
> I might've mentioned BYOD a pair of times in the chapter already. Are you wondering why I am not covering it here? While it's a perfect solution, it has a limitation that, in my opinion, is not a small one: it only allows us to export public data entities. Additionally, the cost of maintaining an Azure SQL instance to host the BYOD infrastructure is much higher than the Data Lake option. However, in a data lake, data is unstructured, and you need to process it to have it available in an SQL database, like what we will do later with Synapse. Keep in mind that this adds some cost.

When the new export to Data Lake functionality was released, we gained a much better way of exporting data because we could finally export single tables, and not only public data entities.

Don't get me wrong; data entities are fine, but if you don't want to do development work, you're constrained to the ones available, and most of the time, they're not enough. Being able to export any of the tables in the system was a big step forward for reporting.

The first version of **Export to Data Lake** used an add-in installed from **Lifecycle Services (LCS)**, but the evolution of the **Export to Data Lake** feature is Azure Synapse Link for Dataverse.

It's also a near real-time integration that will get data from our Dynamics 365 F&O instances into either an Azure Synapse Analytics instance or a data lake, via the linked Dataverse environment to our F&O instance.

What is a data lake?

I think that before learning how to configure an Azure data lake, we should have a brief overview of what a data lake is.

A data lake is like a storage pool where you can place all sorts of data, regardless of its shape or size. Imagine it as a real lake, but instead of water, it's filled with data.

This data can be anything: numbers, texts, videos, images, and more, in any format – organized or not. In our case, the lake will be an Azure storage account.

Additionally, the data lake can not only contain different types of data but also data from different sources. We could have a storage account with data from F&O, but also Dataverse or even non-Microsoft systems.

In a data lake, you don't have to sort or tidy up this data before you store it. You just put it in as it is. And when you need to use some of this data, you can go to the lake, grab it, and then process and analyze it in different ways depending on what you're looking for. This can be done with an Azure Synapse instance, for example.

What is Synapse Link?

Azure Synapse Link is a service that gets data from our data lake, processes it, and converts it from unstructured data in the lake to structured data in the SQL Server instance that is built in the Synapse workspace.

> **Structured versus unstructured data**
>
> Structured data, such as the data available in SQL databases, is organized in a fixed format, such as rows and columns in a spreadsheet, making it easy to search and analyze.
>
> Unstructured data, such as the data we have in a data lake, is not organized in a predefined way and includes formats such as text, images, and videos, which are more complex to process and analyze.

With Synapse Link, we can get our data from F&O into a data lake, and this data will be processed by the Spark pool in the Synapse workspace, which will convert it into SQL format and make it available on the serverless SQL Server pool in the Synapse workspace.

Configuring the Synapse Link integration

The first thing we need to do to configure the data lake integration is create a storage account, a Synapse workspace, and a Spark pool.

First, go to **Storage accounts** and create a new one. You must enable the **Enable hierarchical namespace** option on the **Advanced** tab (see *Figure 8.7*):

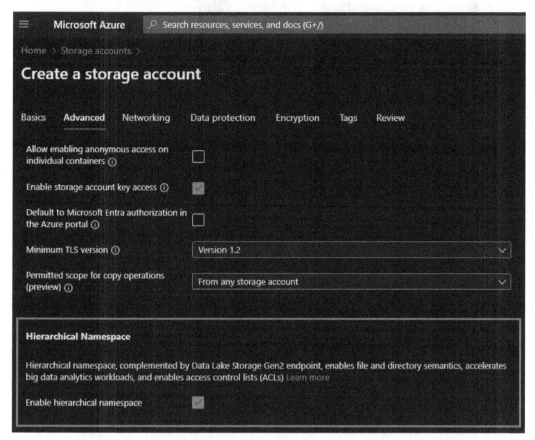

Figure 8.7 – Enable hierarchical namespace option

This is needed for the Data Lake Storage Gen2 functionality to work; otherwise, we can't continue.

Next, we will create an **Azure Synapse Analytics** workspace (see *Figure 8.8*):

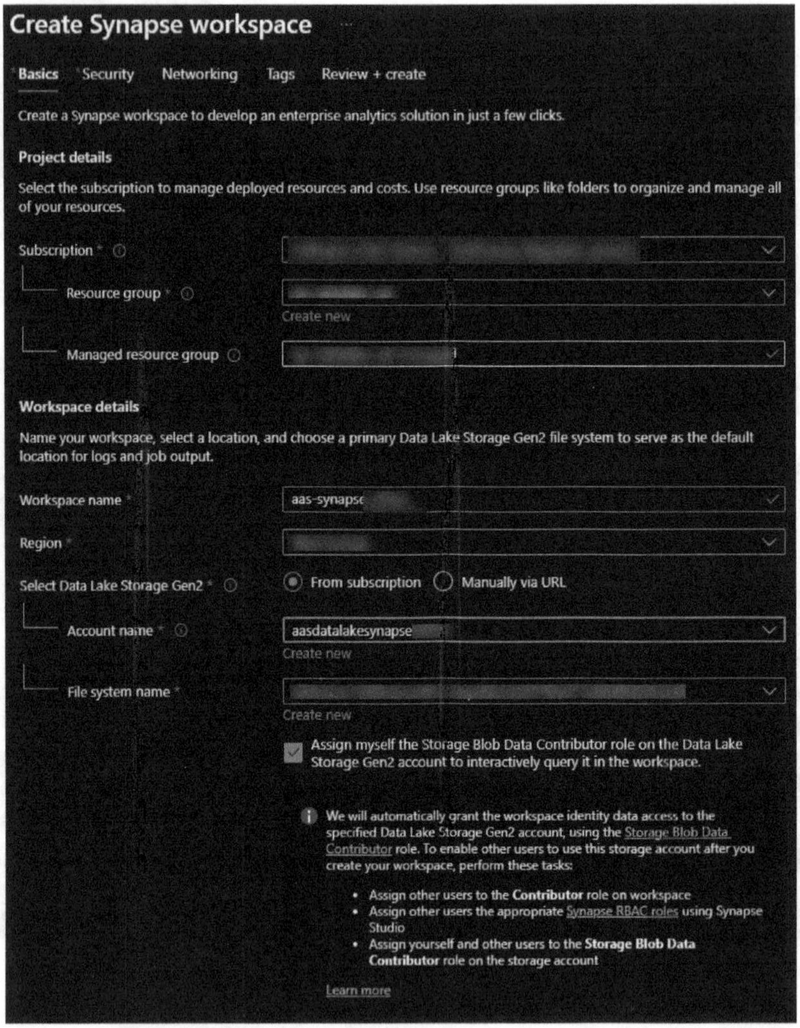

Figure 8.8 – Synapse workspace creation

In the wizard seen in *Figure 8.8*, we have to keep an eye on the following fields:

- **Managed resource group**: This will be a new resource group that will be used by the Synapse workspace. Give it a name, and it will be created.

- **Account name**: The storage account that we created earlier.

- **File system name**: If no filesystem appears after selecting the storage account, create a new one.

Complete the remaining steps and create the resource. When it's ready, we will go back to our storage account and assign the **Storage Blob Data Contributor** role to the managed identity of the workspace.

We can do this in the storage account, under the **Access Control (IAM)** option (see *Figure 8.9*):

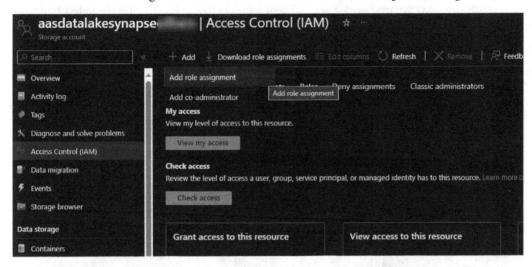

Figure 8.9 – Adding a role assignment to the storage account

Click the **Add** button, then select **Add role assignment**. In the new screen, select the **Storage Blob Data Contributor** role and click **Next**. Switch the **Assign access to** option to **Managed identity** and click the **Select members** link (see *Figure 8.10*):

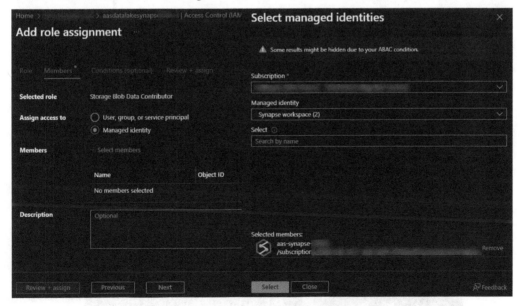

Figure 8.10 – Adding a managed identity

Select your subscription, and under the **Managed identity** dropdown, choose **Synapse workspace**. Your recently deployed Synapse workspace will appear; select it, and finally, click the **Select** button. Finally, assign the role, and we're done.

Now, we will create an Apache Spark pool that will take our unstructured files from the lake and convert them to structured data that will be made available in the SQL Server instance of the workspace (see *Figure 8.11*):

Figure 8.11 – Creating an Apache Spark pool

On the left menu, select the **Apache Spark pools** submenu and create a new pool. Give it a name, select a node size, and fill in the rest of the options. Then go to the **Additional settings** tab where we will select the **Apache Spark** version (see *Figure 8.12*):

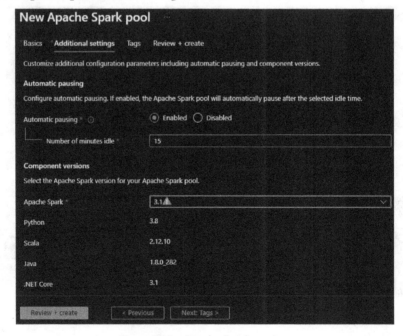

Figure 8.12 – Apache Spark version

At the moment of writing this book, the maximum supported version was 3.1, as shown in the screenshot. Otherwise, the Spark pool won't appear on the wizard when configuring Synapse Link in Dataverse. Finally, create the Spark pool, and we're done on the Azure side.

> **Apache Spark**
>
> **Apache Spark** is an open source tool for processing big data. **Spark** in Synapse Analytics allows for big data processing and can be integrated with other Synapse features such as SQL data warehousing, data exploration, and data ingestion. It provides a unified experience for data prep, data management, data warehousing, big data, and AI tasks. Once all of this is done, we must enable a configuration key in the F&O instance we want to export data from. To do this, you must enable the maintenance mode for the environment in LCS. Then, go to `System administration > Setup > License configuration`.

Now, look for the **Sql row version change tracking** key and enable it (see *Figure 8.13*):

Figure 8.13 – SQL row version change tracking is required

This feature is required because it enables F&O to send incremental synchronization of data to Dataverse, and in the end, allows us to get it into the data lake. Remember to click the **Save** button; a dialog will ask for confirmation. After enabling it, go back to LCS and disable the maintenance mode.

> **Virtual tables**
>
> This functionality requires virtual tables to be available for your environment. This should be already done if you've linked your F&O and Dataverse environments. Otherwise, you can go back to *Chapter 2* and learn how to do it.

The next step is going into the Power Apps maker portal and changing the active environment to the one that's linked to the F&O environment we want to export data from. We also have to enable a feature there to use Synapse Link for F&O. We will do this by navigating to the following URL: `https://make.powerapps.com/environments/YOUR_DATAVERSE_ENVIRONMENT_ID/exporttodatalake?athena.enableFnOTables=true`.

In the preceding URL, you must change `YOUR_DATAVERSE_ENVIRONMENT_ID` to the ID of your own environment. You can find the environment ID on the main environment page in the **Power Platform Admin Center** (**PPAC**).

After that, you should be able to see the **Azure Synapse Link** menu; otherwise, look for it in the left menu. Now, we will create a new link, and a wizard will appear (see *Figure 8.14*):

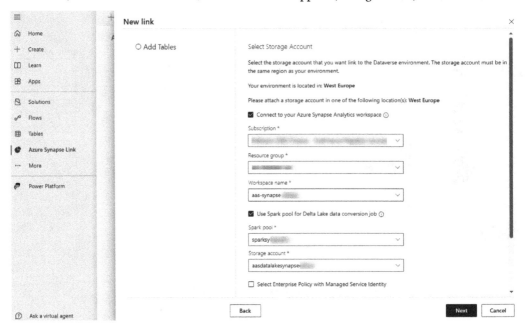

Figure 8.14 – Synapse Link setup

Check the **Connect to your Azure Synapse Analytics workspace** option, then in each of the dropdowns, select the subscription and resource group where you deployed the storage account we created before and the name of the Synapse workspace.

Enable the **Use Spark pool for Delta Lake data conversion job** option, and it should already appear in the Spark pool we just created. The storage account should've already been filled in after selecting the Synapse workspace name; otherwise, fill it in.

Click **Next**, and a list of available tables will appear (see *Figure 8.15*):

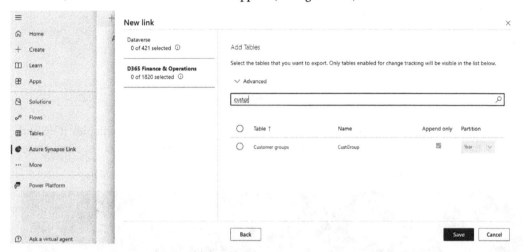

Figure 8.15 – F&O tables in Synapse Link

If you just see Dataverse tables, make sure you've selected the **D365 Finance & Operations** option on the left side of the wizard. Then, you should see the F&O tables and be able to select the ones you want to export. I will go with the **Customer groups** table and click Save.

> **Tip**
> If you get an `Insights Apps Platform Prod` error, wait a few seconds and try again.

Your Synapse Link setup will appear on the maker portal. If you click it, you will see there's an initial sync operation going on (see *Figure 8.16*):

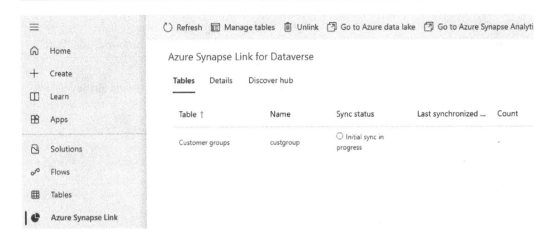

Figure 8.16 – Initial sync in progress

Data is being retrieved into the lake from F&O. Then, the Apache Spark pool will pick it up and convert it to structured SQL data in the Synapse SQL Server instance. This process might take a while.

Now, we will go to our Synapse workspace and open Synapse Studio (see *Figure 8.17*):

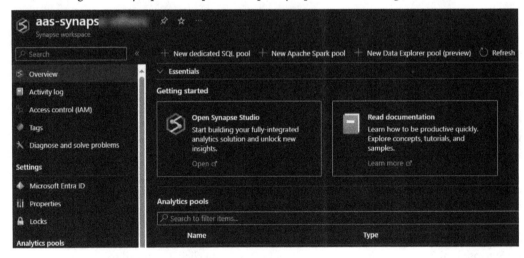

Figure 8.17 – Opening Synapse Studio

Click the **Open** link under the **Getting started** section in the **Overview** submenu. In Synapse Studio, we can browse the SQL Server instance similarly to how we do it in SSMS (see *Figure 8.18*):

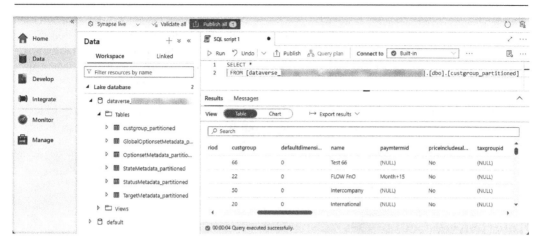

Figure 8.18 – Synapse Studio

If we go to the **Data** menu and expand the database and then the **Tables** node, we will see a table called `custgroup_partitioned`. We can make a SQL `SELECT` query to display the data and see our customer groups in the **Results** window.

As you can see, this is quite an easy way of getting data out of F&O – in my opinion, a much better and flexible one compared to the **Entity Store**. Once we have our data in an SQL Server instance, we can connect Power BI to it and start creating reports!

> **Not only Power BI**
>
> Having our data in a SQL Server instance is useful, not only for Power BI reporting but also for other reporting tools and for external DWH teams that might not be using the Microsoft stack for their BI needs.

Summary

In this chapter, we learned about Power BI dashboards embedded in F&O workspaces, using the **Entity Store** and **Azure Data Lake Storage**. We started with the **Entity Store** in Dynamics 365 F&O, a data store built into the product. This **Entity Store** is used by Power BI dashboards displayed in F&O workspaces, known as analytical workspaces. We also learned how to tackle display errors when these dashboards do not display correctly and how we can refresh **Entity Store** data manually and on a schedule.

We saw the limitations of the **Entity Store** for creating new reports and how using Azure Data Lake integration or Synapse Link instead is much better.

In the last section, we learned to configure Azure Data Lake and Synapse Link, from setting up a storage account and a Synapse workspace to enabling the required configuration in the F&O instance. This offers a more flexible and efficient approach compared to the **Entity Store**, and having data in an SQL Server instance opens possibilities for using various reporting tools beyond Power BI.

Thanks to newer features such as exporting to a data lake or using Synapse Link, we can export any of the tables of the ERP and make them available for our BI teams, enabling them to create better reporting for the needs of the business.

In the next chapter, we'll learn about AI Builder, a low-code AI tool that lets us add AI capabilities to our Power Apps and Power Automate flows.

Questions

You can test your understanding of this chapter by answering the following questions. The answers have been given at the end:

1. What is the primary purpose of the **Entity Store** in Dynamics 365 F&O?

    a. To manage user permissions and roles

    b. To act as a built-in data store used by Power BI dashboards

    c. To provide a platform for custom application development

    d. To serve as a primary database for transaction processing

2. If a Power BI dashboard in Dynamics 365 F&O is not displaying data correctly, what is the likely necessary action?

    a. Upgrading the Dynamics 365 F&O software

    b. Refreshing **Entity Store** data

    c. Reinstalling the Power BI application

    d. Changing the dashboard's data source

3. Which feature is recommended for creating new reports in Dynamics 365 F&O, instead of using the **Entity Store**?

    a. SSMS

    b. Azure Data Lake integration or Synapse Link

    c. BYOD method

    d. Visual Studio development

4. In configuring Azure Data Lake and Synapse Link, what is a crucial step for enabling data export from Dynamics 365 F&O?

    a. Enabling SQL row version change tracking.

    b. Creating a new user in Dynamics 365 F&O.

    c. Installing additional software plugins.

    d. Upgrading the **Entity Store** to the latest version.

5. What advantage does using Azure Data Lake for exporting data offer over the BYOD approach in Dynamics 365 F&O?

    a. It allows only the export of public data entities.

    b. It is more cost-effective and provides broader data access.

    c. It requires less technical expertise to set up.

    d. It exclusively supports Microsoft data formats.

Further reading

To learn more about the topics in this chapter, you can visit the following links.

Power BI integration with Entity store: https://learn.microsoft.com/en-us/dynamics365/fin-ops-core/dev-itpro/analytics/power-bi-integration-entity-store

Resolve issues after entity store maintenance: https://learn.microsoft.com/en-us/dynamics365/fin-ops-core/dev-itpro/analytics/entity-store-maintenance

Create an Azure Synapse Link for Dataverse with Azure Data Lake: https://learn.microsoft.com/en-us/power-apps/maker/data-platform/azure-synapse-link-data-lake

One Dynamics One Platform: Analytics Delta Lake Synapse Link by *Aurélien Clere*: https://www.powerazure365.com/blog-1/one-dynamics-one-platform-analytics-delta-lake-synapse-link

Synapse – Data Lake vs. Delta Lake vs Data Lakehouse: https://techcommunity.microsoft.com/t5/azure-synapse-analytics-blog/synapse-data-lake-vs-delta-lake-vs-data-lakehouse/ba-p/3673653

Answers

1. b. To act as a built-in data store used by Power BI dashboards.
2. b. Refreshing **Entity Store** data.
3. b. Azure Data Lake integration or Synapse Link.
4. a. Enabling SQL row version change tracking.
5. b. It is more cost-effective and provides broader data access.

Part 3: Adding AI to Your Flows and Apps

In this section, we'll learn about AI Builder, examining its nature, the variety of custom and pre-build models it offers, and how to integrate AI Builder into our flows and apps.

This part has the following chapter:

- *Chapter 9, Integrating AI Builder*

9
Integrating AI Builder

Power Platform is not just a set of low-code tools for automation and rapid app development using low-code tools. In this chapter, we're going to learn about AI Builder, a component of Power Platform that helps us add AI capabilities to Power Automate and Power Apps. We can integrate Power Automate flows and Power Apps with AI Builder and use its pre-trained models, which recognize patterns or classify data, to help us speed up and automate repetitive or manual processes.

We will cover the following topics in this chapter:

- AI Builder models
- Adding AI Builder image recognition to Power Automate
- Adding AI Builder image recognition to a Power App

Let's dive into AI Builder and learn about its models!

Technical requirements

In addition to the previous chapter's requirements, for this chapter, you will need AI Builder capacity. If you have a Power Apps, Power Automate, or Dynamics 365 license, you will already have AI Builder credits.

You can also download AI Builder's sample data if you want to follow along when we learn how to train a custom model: `https://learn.microsoft.com/en-us/ai-builder/samples`.

AI Builder models

Before learning about AI Builder's models, let's answer the question, *What is AI Builder?* AI Builder is not a product in Power Platform that can be used alone like the ones we've been learning about so far. Instead, it is a product that adds AI capabilities to other Power Platform products such as Power Automate or Power Apps to help us add AI into everyday business processes in a low-code manner. It makes AI technology accessible and functional for users across various skill levels, particularly those who may not have expertise in not just coding but data science or AI.

The strongest benefit we get from using AI Builder is the ability to close the gap between complex AI algorithms and practical business applications. It integrates with Power Apps, Power Automate, and Power BI, allowing users to add AI capabilities directly into their custom applications, workflows, and data analytics processes (see *Figure 9.1*):

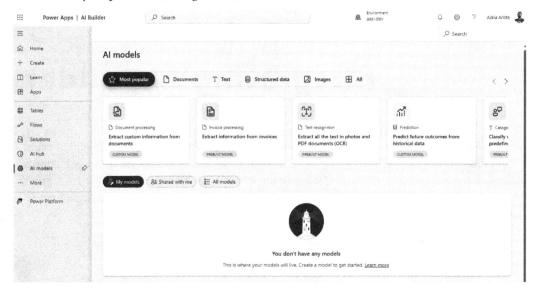

Figure 9.1 – AI Builder models

By providing both prebuilt and custom AI models, AI Builder can cover many business needs and scenarios. Prebuilt models, which are ready for immediate usage, address common business tasks and are ideal for users looking for quick AI integrations. Custom models, on the other hand, offer a higher degree of flexibility but require a more hands-on approach in terms of development and deployment.

Let's learn more about prebuilt and custom AI models!

Prebuilt models

Prebuilt models are ready-to-use AI models that are designed to address common business tasks such as text classification, entity extraction, or sentiment analysis. They require minimal setup and are ideal for businesses seeking quick and efficient AI integrations without the complexity of building models from scratch. The choice between custom and prebuilt models hinges on several factors, including the specificity of the task, available resources, and the desired level of control over the AI model's behavior.

Prebuilt AI models in AI Builder are designed for immediate deployment, addressing common business processes and tasks. These models, which are created and maintained by Microsoft, are trained on diverse datasets, ensuring robust performance across various scenarios.

The different AI Builder prebuilt models we can use in Power Automate or Power Apps are as follows:

- **Invoice processing**: This extracts invoice data such as the invoice ID, date, amount, vendor, and more to help with invoice automation.

- **Text recognition**: This recognizes both printed and handwritten texts.

- **Sentiment analysis**: This labels text as positive, negative, or neutral sentiments, depending on the content of the text.

- **Receipt processing**: This is similar to the text recognition model but focuses on receipts.

- **Entity extraction**: This process recognizes the data that you want to target. Then, it identifies it and classifies it into categories.

- **ID reader**: This identifies the information in identity documents.

- **Key phrase extraction**: This process extracts key data from text.

- **Business card reader**: This is similar to the ID reader model, but it extracts data from business cards instead of ID cards.

- **Category classification**: This classifies texts into categories.

- **Text generation**: This generates text from a prompt the user writes, similar to how ChatGPT does.

- **Language detection**: This process detects the predominant language of a text.

- **Text translation**: This translates text in real time.

- **Image description**: This creates a description from an image, describing what can be seen in the image.

Not everything is as good as it looks!

As you can see, we have several models that will cover many use cases we might want to solve. However, these are not 100% infallible! Take the business card reader model as an example. How many models of business cards can exist? A lot! Each of them with a different design. While the model will hopefully get the data right, it can also fail, so don't trust prebuilt models with your eyes closed.

Additionally, these models can't be modified. If you want something different, you'll have to use a custom model.

Most of these models use **Azure AI Services** (known as Azure Cognitive Services in the past) as their backing service. In F&O, we already have some of them available, such as the invoice processing solution and the expense management add-on, which can be enabled from LCS.

Custom AI models

Custom AI Builder models are ideal for unique business scenarios that might not be covered by the capabilities of the prebuilt models. In this case, you need to train the model before you can use it, but don't panic! This will be done in a low-code manner, just like everything we do on Power Platform.

Imagine that the invoice processing prebuilt model doesn't suit a specific case, where you want to extract more information than what's available out of the box. In this case, you could make use of the document processing AI model, provide enough samples to train it, and use it for that specific case.

But how do you train the model? And is it hard?

As I mentioned previously, there's no need to panic because everything has this low-code flavor that makes it easy to train a model. For instance, there's the image detection model, where you provide an image and AI Builder will detect how many of your desired objects exist in that image. For this example, I will use AI Builder's sample data for the object detection model, which consists of a series of images of tea cans, with different colors for different products.

To train the model, we need to go to the AI Hub inside the maker portal and click the **AI Models** banner. Then, in the model list, we must change to the **Images** selector (see *Figure 9.2*):

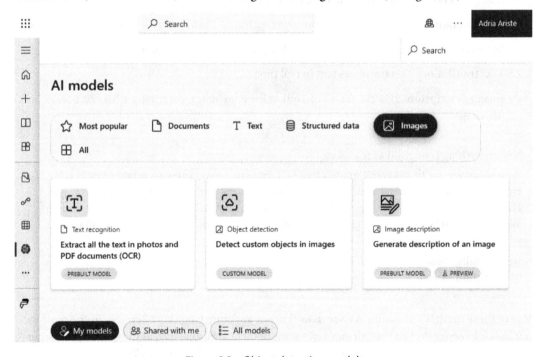

Figure 9.2 – Object detection model

In the model list, select **Detect custom objects in images**. Then, in the dialogue that opens, click **Create custom model**. A wizard will load where we need to select the model domain (see *Figure 9.3*):

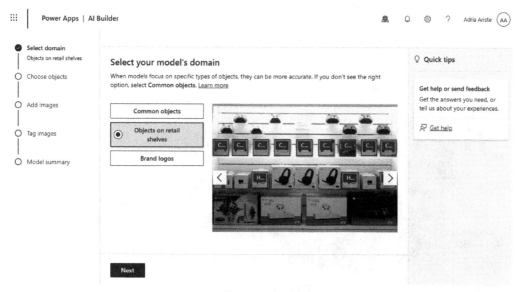

Figure 9.3 – Model domain

For our example, we will select **Objects on retail shelves** and click **Next**. Now, we have to create tags for our objects (see *Figure 9.4*):

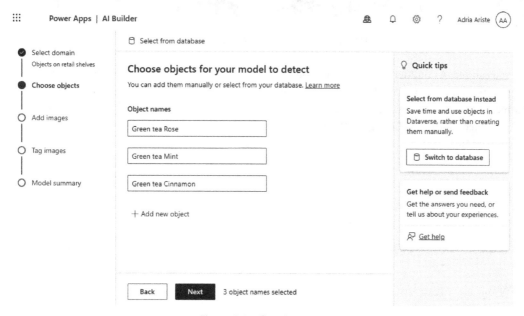

Figure 9.4 – Creating tags

Choosing an object, and adding the different objects as object names, means that for each object that AI Builder needs to identify, we must create a tag or object name. Our sample data has three different tastes of green tea: rose, mint, and cinnamon. So, we have to create a tag for each.

Next, we must upload the images on which we will tag the objects (see *Figure 9.5*):

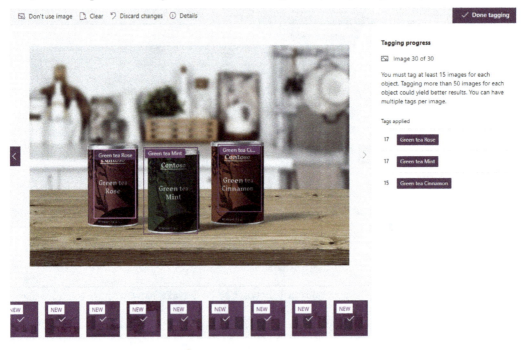

Figure 9.5 – Tagging images for training

As you can see, AI Builder does a pretty good job at identifying objects for tagging, but it doesn't tag them automatically. We can also draw a rectangle around the object and then select which tag is the correct one for it. Keep in mind that for each object you want to identify, you have to tag 15 instances of that object in different images. When we've done that, we can ask AI Builder to train the model (see *Figure 9.6*):

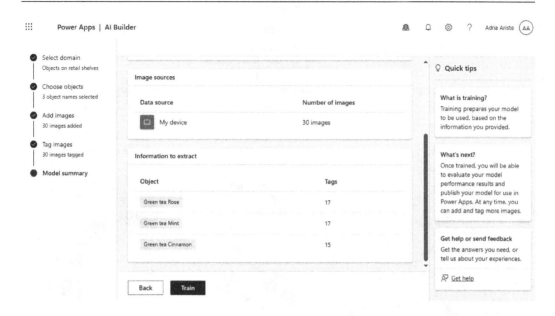

Figure 9.6 – Training the model

To train the model once we've tagged all the images, we have to click the **Train** button. Wait a few minutes; when its status changes to **Trained**, it's ready to be used.

> **AI isn't magic!**
>
> With the latest developments in the field of AI, sometimes, AI looks like magic, but it isn't. AI works on trained data, and if that data is bad, or is tagged incorrectly, our AI solution won't work as we expect.
>
> This means we need to provide enough training data and identify it as expected. AI Builder has a minimum amount of data for each model, but I suggest providing more if possible.

Now, we can perform a quick test by uploading an image from the test folder and seeing the results. How did your model score?

Custom models offer flexibility and specificity but require some resources in terms of data and time. However, thanks to AI Builder, you can see it's not that much data and time!

Adding AI Builder image recognition to Power Automate

Now, let's learn how we can use Power Automate and an image recognition model to update our inventory via email.

Our scenario is as follows: *A warehouse worker will send a weekly picture of a box with oranges in an email. This email will be processed using Power Automate, and AI Builder will count how many oranges are in the box and update the inventory amount in Dynamics 365 F&O.*

To do this, I trained an object detection model with images of oranges, oranges and pineapples, oranges and bananas, and images that contain no oranges. I want to insist on the quality of the data we use to train our models: *our model is only as good as the data we use to create it.*

If we just provide images of oranges, the model will identify all round objects as oranges and you could end up with a bad model (see *Figure 9.7*):

Figure 9.7 – Incorrect identification

In *Figure 9.7*, round fruits are identified as oranges – even bananas! This is because the sample that was used to train the model contained a low variety of images depicting other things that aren't oranges.

Can't find your trained model?

Don't forget to publish the model once you're done training and testing it; otherwise, it won't be available in Power Apps or Power Automate!

Building the flow

We'll start by creating an automated cloud flow in Power Automate. The trigger we'll use is the **When a new email arrives (V3)** one (see *Figure 9.8*):

When a new email arrives (V3)		• • •
Folder	Inbox	🗀
To	AA Adria Ariste ✕	
CC	CC recipient email addresses separated by semicolons (If any matc...	
To or CC	To or CC recipient email addresses separated by semicolons (If any ...	
From	A adria@ariste.dev ✕	
Include Attachments	Yes	⌄
Subject Filter	RECOUNT	
Importance	Any	⌄
Only with Attachments	Yes	⌄

Hide advanced options ⌃

Figure 9.8 – The trigger for our flow

We can add some filters to the trigger so that it only processes some emails, such as looking for the RECOUNT text in the subject. You could also build more complex filters, even using a Dataverse table where you store the allowed senders' email addresses. That's up to you!

Now, we will add a conditional control block to check if the email has an attachment (see *Figure 9.9*):

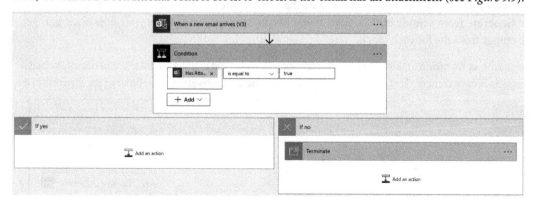

Figure 9.9 – Conditional block to check if any attachment exists

In the comparison, we need to see that the **Has Attachments** output value of the trigger is equal to true. In the **If no** branch, I've also added a **Terminate** action with a status of succeeded to end the execution. In the **If yes** branch, we'll build the logic of our flow.

Because the attachments from the trigger come inside an array (because more than one attachment could exist in the email), the next actions will be inside of a for each loop. First, we will retrieve the current item of the attachments and parse it with the **Parse JSON** action we used in previous chapters (see *Figure 9.10*):

Figure 9.10 – Parse JSON

Remember that we can automatically generate the **Schema** property that the parse action needs using the **Generate from sample** button. Also, if you need a sample, you can run your flow once, and get the output from the for each block.

The attachment comes in a base64 string. We cannot pass this string to the AI Builder action directly because it expects binary content. That's why we have to convert the base64 string into binary (see *Figure 9.11*):

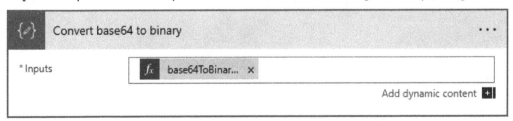

Figure 9.11 – Convert base64 to binary

We can accomplish this using the built-in `base64ToBinary` function in Power Automate with the `contentBytes` element of the parsed JSON. The formula will look like this:

```
base64ToBinary(body('Parse_JSON')?['contentBytes'])
```

Now, we can add an AI Builder action of the **Detect and count objects in images** type (see *Figure 9.12*):

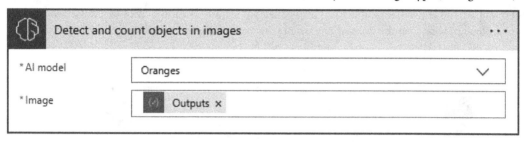

Figure 9.12 – AI Builder action

In the **AI model** field, we have to select the model that we created and trained previously. In the **Image** field, we must place the output of the **Convert base64 to binary** action.

This will send the image to our AI Builder model, process it, and return a JSON array with an element for each object detected successfully. This means we need to count the number of items of that array and, if there are any, continue (see *Figure 9.13*):

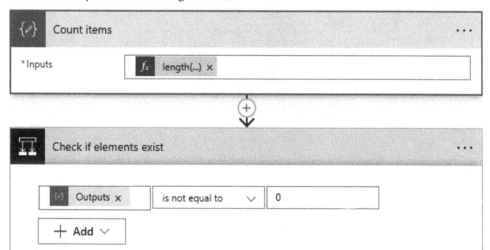

Figure 9.13 – Conditional block to check if any object was detected

To count the items, we can use the `length` function, like this:

```
length(outputs('Detect_and_count_objects_in_images')?['body/
responsev2/predictionOutput/results'])
```

Once we know that the array is not empty, which means there are some elements inside it, we can add a conditional action and only continue if the value is different than 0; this means that objects were detected. At this point, we can continue with the adjustment journal creation in Dynamics 365 F&O (see *Figure 9.14*).

But wait – the count could also be 0 if we had no items available, right? Yes, of course! We could have run out of articles and had 0 quantity on the journal, but I wanted to show cases where we have some value instead of what is in the journal line when you create it!

Figure 9.14 – Journal creation in F&O

To create the journal in F&O from Power Automate, I'm using the `InventoryAdjustmentJournalEntriesV2` entity, which creates both the journal header and lines. Then in the **Quantity** field, I set the value of counting the items in the array that AI Builder returns.

Because I'm using Microsoft's demo Contoso data, I'm providing the item number, site and warehouse dimensions, and the name of the journal as plain text because this is an example. As I mentioned earlier, we could create a Dataverse table to parameterize all of these values, depending on the address and subject of the email that triggers this process.

Testing the flow

I will send an email with an attachment of an image with three oranges. This should trigger the flow, process the image, and create the journal (see *Figure 9.15*):

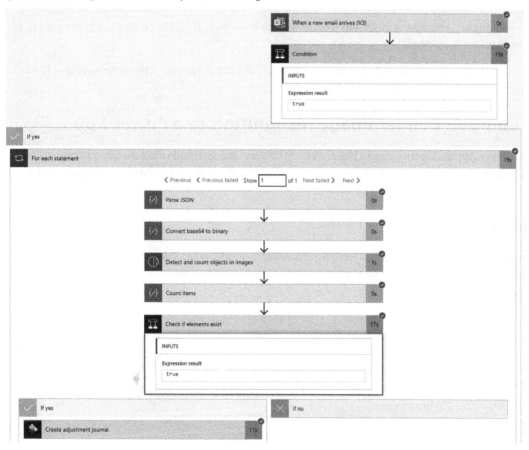

Figure 9.15 – Successfully executed flow

As we can see, all the steps have been completed. In the first condition, we found an attachment and processed it, while in the second condition, we checked that objects were found in the image and created a journal in F&O (see *Figure 9.16*):

Figure 9.16 – Journal created in F&O

As you can see, this new adjustment journal says that for item D0007, on site 1, warehouse 11, 3 units have been counted.

This is one way of achieving this automated counting, but what if we wanted to do the same in a Power App? Let's learn how to do it!

Adding AI Builder image recognition to a Power App

The Power App that we're going to build here will be very simple: it will contain a list of items for your user company, and you will be able to select an item and then use your camera to do an inventory adjustment of that item using AI Builder!

Building the app

To do this, we will use the virtual table for the released products (EcoResProductV2Entity); make sure it's enabled before you start! Rename the screen ItemList and add a vertical gallery (see *Figure 9.17*):

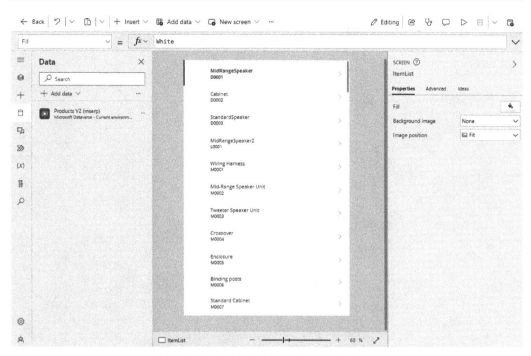

Figure 9.17 – Vertical gallery showing the items

I've removed the image element from the gallery. Set the **Products V2** entity as the data source, and edit the fields. As the title, I'll be using the product name, and then the product number as the subtitle. Next, create a variable called `SelectedItem`. Remember that to do this, we must select the **App** node from the left pane, and in the `OnStart` property, we must add the following formula:

```
Set(SelectedItem, "");
```

This creates the variable with an empty value. We will use it to save which item we want to do the recount for. Create a new screen and name it `Details`. Go back to the **ItemList** screen and select the **NextArrow1** element of the gallery (see *Figure 9.18*):

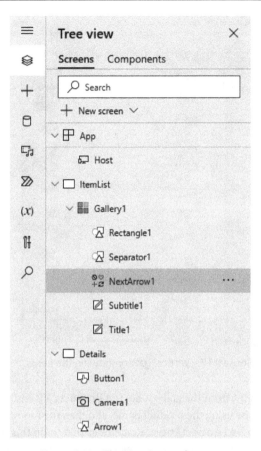

Figure 9.18 – The NextArrow element

The **NextArrow1** element shown in *Figure 9.18* is the > arrow we can see on the left-hand side of each line in the gallery (see *Figure 9.17*). We will use it as a button to navigate to the **Details** screen. On its OnSelect property, add this formula:

Set(SelectedItem, Gallery1.Selected.'Product number');Navigate(Details);

Here, we're saving the current element's product number into the SelectedItem variable, and then changing to the **Details** screen. Now, we can go to the **Details** screen.

Add the AI Builder component for **Object detector** and select your AI model – the one we created in the previous section. Name it ObjectDetector. Next, create the following objects:

- A button named CreateBtn
- A label named DetectedLbl with the text Detected objects:
- A label named DetectedNumLbl with an empty text box

Now, select the AI Builder component. For OnChange, set this formula:

```
Set(DetectedItems, ObjectDetector.GroupedResults);
```

This will create a variable called DetectedItems and store the results of the image processing in it. The GroupedResults field will make the DetectedItems variable of the table type because that's what GroupResults are and the variable sets its type depending on what we assign to it first. Now, we're going to use it in the DetectedNumLbl label. In its Text property, add this formula:

```
First(DetectedItems).ObjectCount
```

Because the DetectedItems variable is a table, we have to retrieve a specific record before selecting any field and returning it. We will only have a single record in the variable because each time the processing runs, it overwrites the value of the DetectedItems variable. From that record, we return the ObjectCount value, which will be displayed as the text of the label. Your app should look like this (see *Figure 9.19*):

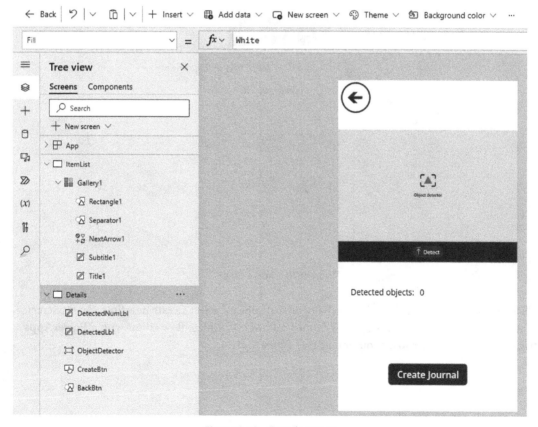

Figure 9.19 – Details screen

You will see the back button on top, the AI Builder component in the center, and below that the `DetectedLbl` label (with the text **Detected objects**) and next to it the `DetectedNumLbl` label. Finally, you have the button on the bottom.

Creating the journal

We just need to do one more thing, which is create a Power Automate flow that will be called from the button and that will create the journal in Dynamics 365 F&O. To do this, change to **Power Automate** from the left pane (see *Figure 9.20*):

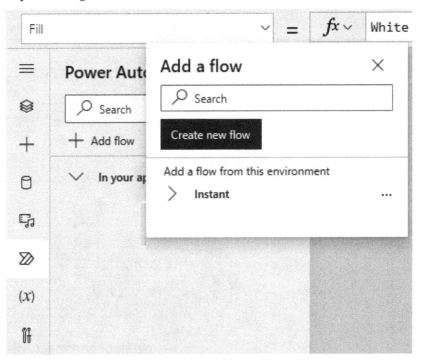

Figure 9.20 – Add a flow

Click the **Add flow** button. Then, in the dialogue that appears, select **Create new flow**. On the screen that opens, select **Create a flow**. This will open a Power Automate flow editor with a **PowerApps** trigger to which we have to add our inputs (see *Figure 9.21*):

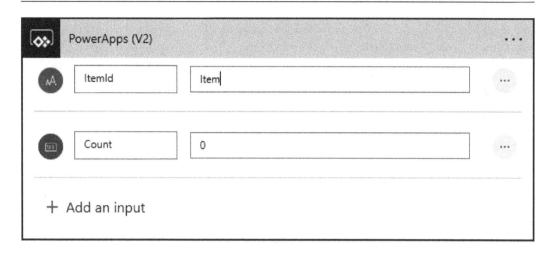

Figure 9.21 – PowerApps trigger with inputs

We need two things to update the inventory quantity of an item: the item number and the quantity. So, create a string input and call it ItemId, and a number input and call it Count.

Now, as we did previously, we will add a condition to check if the value of Count is 0, and, if it isn't, continue with the process (see *Figure 9.22*):

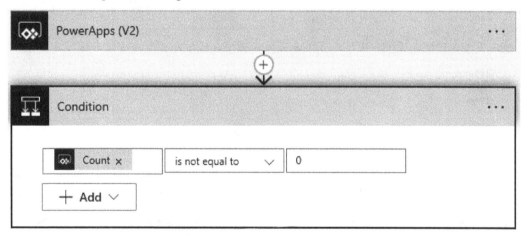

Figure 9.22 – Checking that Count is not 0

To do this, just check that the Count value is not equal to 0. As I mentioned previously, we could have scenarios where we want the flow to run even if it's 0, but I want to show greater values.

In the **If yes** branch, add an F&O **Create record** action that uses the `InventoryAdjustment-JournalEntriesV2` entity again (see *Figure 9.23*):

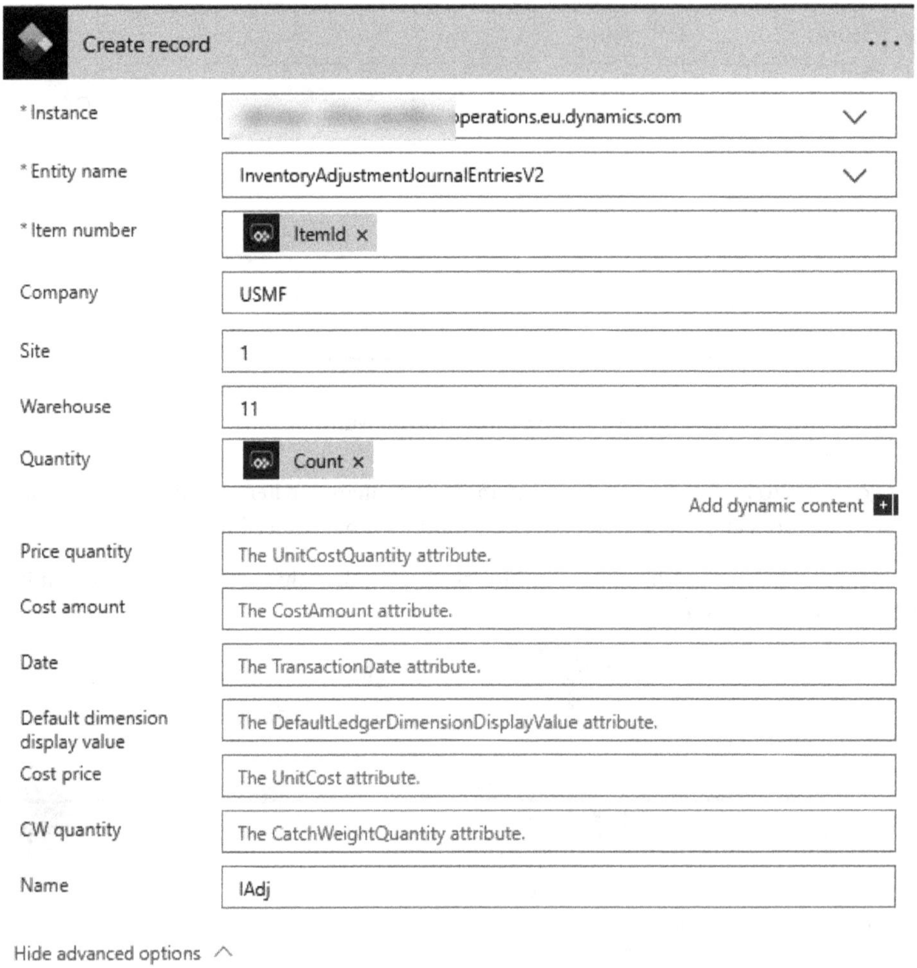

Figure 9.23 – The Create record action

We use the input values from the trigger in the **Item** number and **Quantity** fields and complete the required fields, such as **Site** or **Warehouse**. Rename the flow `CreateJournal` and save and close it.

Back in the Power Apps designer, select the button's `OnSelect` property and call the flow, like this:

```
CreateJournal.Run(SelectedItem, DetectedNumLbl.Txt);
```

We added two input fields to the trigger, so we need to pass two values in the Run method. The first one is the product number in the `SelectedItem` variable, and the second one is the number of objects that were counted in the image using the value of the label's `DetectedNumLbl.Text` property.

Testing the app

Run the app. From the list that appears, select an item (oranges, in my case – see *Figure 9.24*):

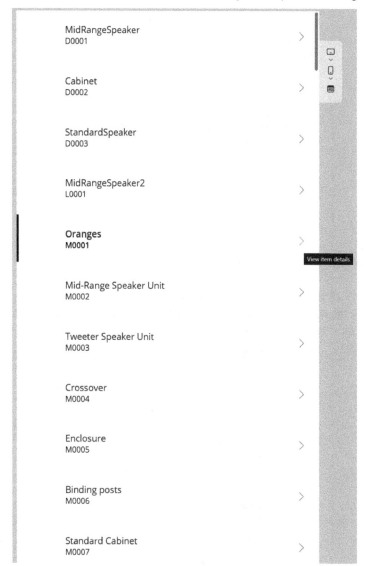

Figure 9.24 – Item list in Power Apps

To go to the **Details** screen, click on the right arrow on the right-hand side of the screen. On the **Details** screen, click the **Detect** button on the **Object detector** component and take or upload a picture of the item (see *Figure 9.25*):

Figure 9.25 – Adding an image to detect

As shown in *Figure 9.25*, this will send the image to the AI Builder model and return the results. When it's back, we will see the number of objects that were detected and we can click on the **Create Journal** button. This will trigger the flow (see *Figure 9.26*):

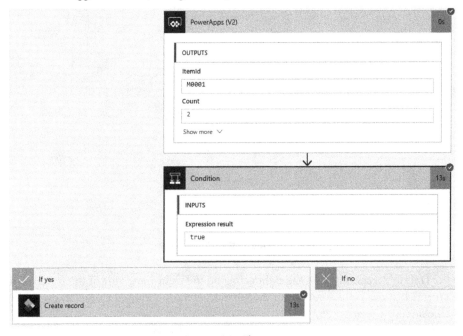

Figure 9.26 – Flow run

Here, we can see that the inputs are **ItemId** number M0001 and **Count** 2 and that the flow has run the action of creating the F&O record successfully. Go to the inventory adjustment journals and check the one that's been created (see *Figure 9.27*):

Figure 9.27 – Inventory journal created in F&O

We can see a line for M0001 and a quantity of 2. Success! Our Power App now allows warehouse workers to quickly update the inventory with a single picture and a well-trained AI model.

I want to stress this one more time: *the success of your AI model, and the rate of correct identification, depends on the quality and quantity of the data you use to train it.*

With that, you've learned how to use AI Builder with a custom model to add AI to your Power Automate flows or Power Apps.

Summary

In this chapter, we learned how AI Builder can help us build AI into Power Platform applications such as Power Automate and Power Apps, which offers advantages in automating and enhancing business processes through AI. AI Builder is a component of Power Platform that allows users of varying skill levels to incorporate AI into their workflows with minimal or no coding.

We saw that it offers both prebuilt and custom AI models: prebuilt models are ready to use for common tasks such as text and image recognition, sentiment analysis, and data extraction, while custom models provide more flexibility and can be tailored for specific business needs. We also familiarized ourselves with the fact that training custom AI models in AI Builder is a low-code process.

Next, we learned how AI Builder models can be integrated into Power Automate flows and Power Apps. For instance, a Power Automate flow can be designed to use an image recognition model to update inventory in Dynamics 365 F&O. This involves training a model to recognize specific objects (oranges, in our example), then using Power Automate to process images sent via email, count the objects, and update inventory data accordingly. This method demonstrates the practical application of AI in automating inventory management tasks.

Similarly, AI Builder can enhance Power Apps by adding AI-driven functionalities. A simple Power App can be built to assist in inventory management, where the app lists items and allows users to select an item and adjust its inventory using AI Builder's object detection capabilities. Users can take a photo of the item; the app, powered by the custom AI model, will count the items and update the inventory. This process highlights the ease and efficiency of incorporating AI into business applications, thus significantly simplifying tasks such as inventory management.

In the next chapter, we will learn about the Power Platform admin center, where we can manage the Dataverse environments, and soon also the F&O environments!

Questions

Now, it's time to check what you've learned in this chapter. Go ahead and answer these questions!

1. What is the primary function of AI Builder in Power Platform?

    a. To provide advanced coding capabilities

    b. To add AI capabilities to Power Platform products

    c. To replace the need for Power Automate and Power Apps

    d. To solely manage Dynamics 365 licenses

2. Which of the following is a key advantage of using prebuilt AI models in AI Builder?

    a. They require advanced coding skills for setup

    b. They are not ready for immediate deployment

    c. They address common business tasks with minimal setup

    d. They are less accurate than custom models

3. What is necessary when training a custom AI model in AI Builder?

    a. Extensive programming knowledge

    b. A high-cost licensing fee

    c. Tagging a significant number of samples

    d. A degree in data science

4. In the Power Automate flow we created, how is AI Builder used for inventory management?

   a. It creates financial reports

   b. It automatically writes emails

   c. It counts objects in images to update inventory

   d. It schedules meetings based on inventory levels

5. What is a critical factor for the accuracy of a custom AI model in AI Builder?

   a. The color scheme of the Power App interface

   b. The number of users accessing the model

   c. The quality and quantity of the training data

   d. The speed of the internet connection

Further reading

To learn more about the topics that were covered in this chapter, take a look at the following resources:

Overview of AI Builder: `https://learn.microsoft.com/en-us/ai-builder/overview`

Overview of prebuilt AI models: `https://learn.microsoft.com/en-us/ai-builder/prebuilt-overview`

AI Builder in Power Automate: `https://learn.microsoft.com/en-us/ai-builder/use-in-flow-overview`

AI Builder in Power Apps: `https://learn.microsoft.com/en-us/ai-builder/use-in-powerapps-overview`

AI Builder labs: `https://learn.microsoft.com/en-us/ai-builder/learn-ai-builder`

Sample data: `https://learn.microsoft.com/en-us/ai-builder/samples`

Answers

1. a. To add AI capabilities to Power Platform products
2. c. They address common business tasks with minimal setup
3. c. Tagging a significant number of samples
4. c. It counts objects in images to update inventory
5. c. The quality and quantity of the training data

Part 4: Dataverse and Power Platform ALM

In this part, we'll learn how we manage Dataverse environments and the different types of environments we can use. We will also learn about ALM using solutions and how we can use these solutions to move the components we create between environments.

This part has the following chapters:

- *Chapter 10, Environment Management*
- *Chapter 11, Solution Management*

10

Environment Management

As Dynamics 365 **Finance and Operations** (**F&O**) consultants, we're used to managing our environments in **Lifecycle Services** (**LCS**). Managing Dataverse environments is done from the **Power Platform admin center** (**PPAC**), where we can also check usage information. In this chapter, we will learn about the different types of environments and PPAC. This is something we'll need to be familiar with in the near future as PPAC will also become the place where F&O environments are managed. Also, while that doesn't happen, we need to understand how Dataverse environments are displayed in PPAC.

We will explore the following topics in this chapter:

- F&O and Dataverse environments
- Environment types

F&O and Dataverse environments

While this may seem something that's not related to F&O, it's something that Dynamics 365 consultants will need to be familiar with, and not only if you want to configure F&O and Dataverse environment linking. Why?

In the near future, LCS is going to be replaced by PPAC, and existing projects will be migrated to PPAC over the coming years until LCS is finally deprecated. All customers onboarding a Dynamics 365 F&O project will be using the new experience in PPAC, deploying and managing environments from there instead of LCS.

> **Goodbye LCS!**
>
> While new customers will only use PPAC, existing customers will still be using LCS. However, they will be migrated to PPAC, and finally, LCS will be retired.

The new unified developer experience, where a F&O environment is deployed from Dataverse to be used for development, is also a hint of what the future of F&O in PPAC looks like (see *Figure 10.1*):

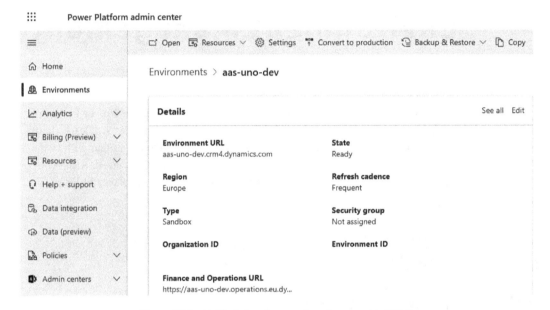

Figure 10.1 – Unified development environment in PPAC

After deploying the environment, we will have a Dataverse environment, with its classic CRM URL (at the top of the **Details** section), but also an F&O environment that we can access with its own URL (at the bottom of the **Details** section). This environment won't appear on LCS, and this will happen with all the environments created from PPAC in the future.

But before all these changes happen, it's better to learn about the different elements of PPAC.

When we log in to PPAC at `https://admin.powerplatform.microsoft.com/`, we will see the left sidebar with several menu items (see *Figure 10.2*):

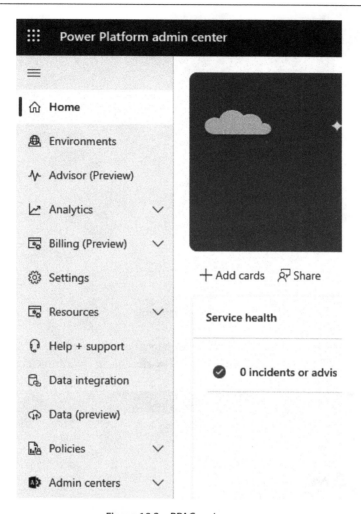

Figure 10.2 – PPAC main menu

Let's see which items are the most interesting for people working with Dataverse and F&O.

Environments

On the **Environments** page, we will see a list of all the environments we have access to (see *Figure 10.3*):

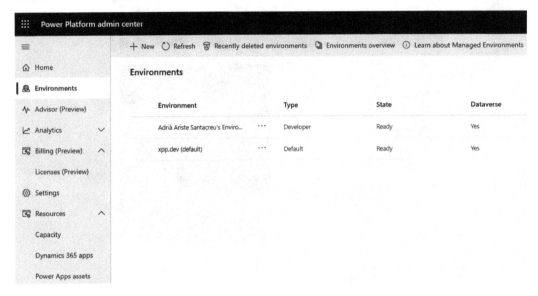

Figure 10.3 – Environments list on PPAC

In *Figure 10.3*, we can see two environments and some options on the top bar, and for each environment, there are some properties in the **Environments** list. If we click on an environment name, we will see its details (see *Figure 10.4*):

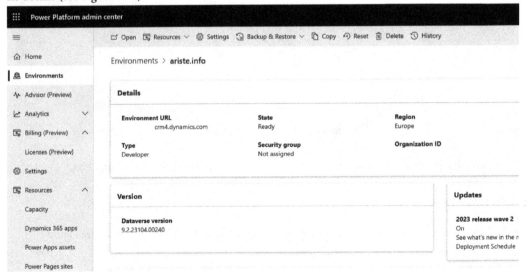

Figure 10.4 – Environment details

On the **Details** page, we can see the environment's URL, type, region, organization, and so on. The options on the menu at the top change when we select an environment, and we can perform the following actions:

- **Open**: Navigate to the base URL of the environment.

- **Resources**: It contains four options in the submenu:

  - **Dynamics 365 apps**: See which Dynamics 365 apps are installed on the environment.

  - **Power Pages sites**: See which Power Pages sites are created in the environment.

  - **Power Apps**: See the Power Apps created in the environment.

  - **Flows**: See the Power Automate flows created in the environment.

- **Settings**: View or modify environment settings, such as users, feature management, logging, integrations, and so on.

- **Backup & Restore**: Perform backup and restore operations on the environment.

- **Copy**: Copy the environment to another one. You can choose to copy everything (including data) or just customizations.

- **Reset**: Delete and redeploy the environment. This operation can only be triggered in sandbox environments.

- **Delete**: Delete the environment.

- **History**: List the operations that have taken place in the environment.

And now, we go back to the **Environments** list. Notice one of the environments has the type **Default** and also (default) as part of its name (see *Figure 10.5*)?

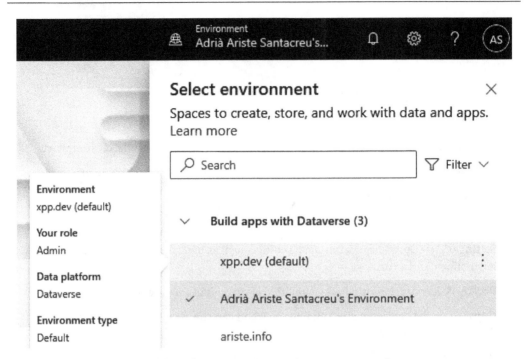

Figure 10.5 – Default environment in the environment selector

As you may have guessed, the environment with the (default) suffix is the default environment. And now, we need to learn some things about it.

All tenants have a default environment, and all users in the tenant have access to the default environment. This means you can create an app, data, or a flow in it without having to ask for permission to access it. And that can be you… or anyone in your organization!

Of course, there's a way of fixing this, which is assigning a **Microsoft Entra ID** (known before as Azure Active Directory) security group to the default environment, and only users in that group will be able to access it.

Furthermore, we cannot perform backup and recovery operations in PPAC for the default environment! Any important or business-critical data you place there is not safe.

> **I truly mean it; don't use it!**
>
> If you open the Power Platform maker portal and only see your tenant's default environment in the **Environments** list, don't use it to create Power Apps or Power Automate flows. Even if you just want to use it for testing, it's better to contact your PPAC admin and ask them to deploy a new environment.

Resources

On the **Resources** menu, we have four options:

- **Capacity**
- **Dynamics 365 apps**
- **Power Apps assets**
- **Power Pages sites**

The most interesting one for us will be the **Capacity** one, and we will focus on this one. It has several tabs, but we will focus on the **Dataverse** and **Finance and operations** ones (see *Figure 10.6*):

Figure 10.6 – Dataverse capacity tab

On the **Dataverse** capacity tab, we can check the current database, file, and log usage of each environment. Similarly, on the **Finance and operations** tab, we can see the F&O database and file usage; not the Dataverse space used, but the F&O database – the old AxDB!

If you're a global admin, Dataverse admin, or Dynamics 365 admin, you can also see a summarized view of all storage capacity across Dataverse and F&O.

> **Watch your capacity!**
> For both Dataverse and F&O, the capacity you have on your tenant depends on the number of licenses you have purchased, especially for F&O. Make sure you check the licensing guide for more details! The licensing information is updated monthly.

Now, let's learn more about environment types – except the default one.

Environment and project planning

This is an important part of a project and is something you must evaluate and plan before starting any work. I'd even say that it would be extremely positive if you could plan this before starting the F&O or Dataverse implementation project, and ideally, if you know you will be using both systems in your company or customer, it's something you should do during the first stages of analysis.

> **Remember this!**
>
> We can only have *ONE* Dataverse environment linked to a F&O environment. For example, it's not possible to use F&O's virtual tables from different Dataverse environments. If you have a scenario such as that, you will have to go with an alternative solution, such as using middleware software.

If your project doesn't include any Dynamics 365 app on Dataverse (Sales, Marketing, and so on) and you just want to benefit from using Dataverse and Power Platform in your F&O implementation, you can safely configure the Power Platform integration.

If in the future, the company decides to start using – for example – Dynamics 365 Sales, it will need Dataverse environments. In this case, you will have to work with the team implementing the Dataverse apps and keep in mind that you already have Dataverse environments in use with F&O. You must evaluate if you want to build any integration using Dual-write or virtual tables, and if it's the case, using the existing Dataverse environments.

If your project includes both ERP and CRM apps, and you plan on using Dual-write and/or virtual tables, you need to work with both teams, meet with them, and plan what your environments will look like. Even with the convergence plans, the **application lifecycle management** (**ALM**) of F&O and Dataverse projects might be a bit different, and you want to align both teams for a successful outcome of the project.

> **Unicorns only exist in books**
>
> As an ERP consultant, regardless of whether you are a technical or functional consultant, you already know that it's very hard to find someone who has a very high knowledge of all the modules in the ERP. And with the number of new functionalities published with each release wave, it's becoming even harder.
>
> Regarding Dataverse, you don't need to know it all, but I strongly suggest learning the basics, and if you're an architect learning about environment management and planning, it is, in my opinion, a must.

Now, let's learn about the different environment types in Dataverse and how they relate to those in F&O.

Environment types

As in F&O, Dataverse has different environment types depending on their purpose. In Dynamics 365 F&O, we have:

- Production environment
- Sandbox environments
- Development environments

One production and one sandbox environment are included with the initial license purchase and are deployed in a Microsoft-owned subscription. You can buy additional sandbox environments, known as add-on sandbox environments. These environments are maintained and serviced by Microsoft.

The F&O development environments are Azure virtual machines deployed in your or your customer's Azure subscription. The responsibility of maintaining these environments is yours, or your customer's.

Likewise, in Dataverse, we can have production, sandbox, and developer environments. The purpose of each environment is similar to those of F&O.

> **Dataverse is special**
> In F&O, we have a single production environment, and it makes sense for it to be like that. But Dataverse is different, and you can have more than one production environment in the same tenant!

Additionally, we can deploy trial environments, as we learned in *Chapter 2*!

Linked environments

If we're working on a project where we have linked environments, you will most likely see the same number of environments in PPAC as the ones you've configured through the Power Platform integration on LCS. But we could also have more environments; for example, if we also have a CRM project going on, we may have other sandbox environments being used by the Power Platform team to do development or testing work.

So, in your F&O and Power Platform implementation project, you should at least have:

- One **production** environment on the F&O side and one on the Dataverse side. These will be the ones used by the users to do their daily work.
- One or more **sandbox** environments for F&O and Dataverse. These sandbox environments can be used for user testing, pre-production, integration testing, and so on.

> **Consider deployments to production!**
>
> Remember that on the F&O side, we have a constraint when updating production: we first need to deploy the changes to a sandbox environment. Plan this with the Dataverse team!

We have sandbox environments that we can compare directly to F&O's sandbox environments. They're used for non-production tasks, such as testing or development, as we've just seen.

And finally, the production environment, where we deploy all our solutions once tested, and the end users do the real work.

And what about development environments? Well, that will be a bit different from what F&O developers are used to!

Developer environments

If you're an F&O developer, you probably expect that Dataverse development is done on the developer type of environment, right? Well, it may not be like that because Dataverse development is usually done in sandbox environments.

The developer-type environment is related to the newer **Power Apps Developer Plan**, which gives you a free development environment to create apps, flows, or use Dataverse capabilities. It has a limit of 750 flow runs per month and 2 GB of database space. So, as you can imagine, for some organizations, it's not enough.

This is why Dataverse sandbox environments are normally used for development and testing. For example, if you have an F&O development environment that has the Power Platform integration configured, you can go and check that the Dataverse environment that was created when you deployed the F&O development environment is of type sandbox!

It might sound a bit counterintuitive for F&O folks, but remember: even though they have the same base name – Dynamics 365 – they're two different products!

Summary

In this chapter, we've learned about Dataverse environments and how they are related to F&O when the link between them is configured. We've also seen that in the future, the old way of doing things with LCS is getting phased out and it'll be all about PPAC. This change will be important for consultants in this space because they need to get the hang of using PPAC for everything, from setting up to managing these environments.

In PPAC, we've got a bunch of tools at our fingertips. We can see details of each environment, such as its URL and type, check which Dynamics 365 apps are installed, tweak settings, back up and restore, and even delete environments if we need to.

We've also seen we have the default environment in Dataverse. Everyone has access to it, which can be a bit risky, especially since you can't back it up in PPAC. So, if you're just messing around or testing, better ask your admin to set you up with a different environment.

Then, we learned about the importance of environment planning. If you're working on a project that uses both F&O and Dataverse, you've got to plan carefully. You can only link one Dataverse environment to an F&O environment, so any integration you're thinking about, such as using Dual-write or virtual tables, needs to be thought out well in advance.

Lastly, the chapter talks about different types of environments in both F&O and Dataverse. You've got production, sandbox, and development environments. Each has its own purpose and setup. For example, in Dataverse, you can have multiple production environments, which is not the case with F&O. If you're working on a project that combines both, you need to sync up with everyone involved to make sure things go smoothly. And remember: whether you're more into the technical or functional side of things, getting a grip on the basics of Dataverse and environment management is super important.

In the next chapter, we'll learn about solutions, where we create our flows and apps, and use them to move changes between environments.

Questions

Now, it's time to test your knowledge about this chapter and Dataverse environments with the following questions:

1. What will be replacing LCS for managing F&O environments?

    a. Azure DevOps

    b. Power BI Admin Center

    c. PPAC

    d. Microsoft Teams admin center

2. Which of the following cannot be performed on the default environment in PPAC?

    a. Checking the environment's URL

    b. Performing manual backup and restore operations

    c. Accessing all tenant users

    d. Viewing the environment's type and region

3. What should you monitor in PPAC to manage resources effectively?

    a. User activity logs

    b. Storage capacity

    c. Number of environment deployments

    d. Frequency of environment access

4. In a project involving both F&O and Dataverse, how many Dataverse environments can be linked to a single F&O environment?

    a. One

    b. Two

    c. Three

    d. Unlimited

5. What type of environment is typically used for Dataverse development?

    a. Production environment

    b. Sandbox environment

    c. Developer environment

    d. Trial environment

Further reading

To learn more about this chapter, you can visit the following links:

Microsoft Power Platform adoption best practices: https://learn.microsoft.com/en-us/power-platform/guidance/adoption/methodology

Manage the default environment: https://learn.microsoft.com/en-us/power-platform/guidance/adoption/manage-default-environment

Finance and operations storage capacity: https://learn.microsoft.com/en-us/power-platform/admin/finance-operations-storage-capacity

Create and manage environments in the Power Platform admin center: https://learn.microsoft.com/en-us/power-platform/admin/create-environment

About the Power Apps Developer Plan: https://learn.microsoft.com/en-us/power-platform/developer/plan

Answers

1. c. PPAC
2. b. Performing manual backup and restore operations
3. b. Storage capacity
4. a. One
5. b. Sandbox environment

11

Solution Management

If you've been following the samples in this book, you've maybe created Power Automate flows and Power Apps as standalone components instead of as part of a solution. That's not a best practice, and in this chapter, we'll learn about solutions and how we can use them to move our components between different environments.

We will also learn about the different types of solutions and how we can use environment variables to reduce manual setup when moving solutions between environments.

In this chapter, we will cover the following topics:

- Why do we need solutions?
- Exporting and importing solutions

Why do we need solutions?

If you're familiar with X++, or also .NET development, you may know the concept of a **solution** or **project** (see *Figure 11.1*):

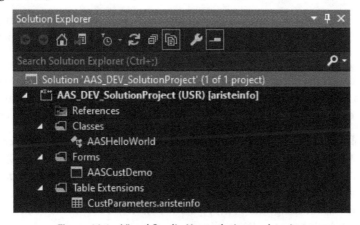

Figure 11.1 – Visual Studio X++ solution and project

In X++, we use Visual Studio projects to group objects that we create. We customize existing objects in the system or create new functionalities. Likewise, in Power Platform, we can use solutions (see *Figure 11.2*):

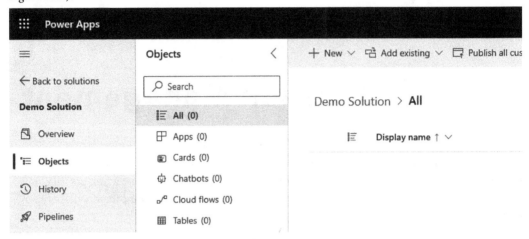

Figure 11.2 – Power Platform solution

In solutions, which you can access in the maker portal, we can group components (such as apps, flows, or tables) that we create in Dataverse. We will later use these solutions to move changes between environments.

Let's start with learning what ALM is, why it is important, and what it has to do with solutions!

ALM

ALM, which stands for **application lifecycle management**, is the life-cycle management of applications. I know – I just used the same words to try to explain a concept; let me explain better.

Imagine you're building a house. ALM is the set of tools and practices you use to manage the entire process – from the initial idea of building a house, designing, building, and maintaining it, and even renovating it.

In software, ALM covers the life of an application from its conception, through its development and deployment, to its eventual retirement. It's like the toolbox that helps software teams manage and track the progress of software development, ensuring that everything stays organized and on track.

For F&O, these tools can include **Lifecycle Services** (**LCS**), the **Power Platform admin center** (**PPAC**), Azure DevOps, or Visual Studio. When the project starts, we use LCS (and soon PPAC) to deploy the environments, add users to the project, and configure the link to Azure DevOps. Then, development work is done in Visual Studio, and we check the code in Azure DevOps, where it is also automatically built if you have **continuous integration** (**CI**) pipelines and released to the sandbox environments if you have **continuous deployment** (**CD**) pipelines.

ALM tools provide a structured framework for all these stages, helping teams communicate better, stay organized, and ensure quality at every step. When working with Power Platform, we also have ALM tools, and solutions will be the base of it for us.

> **It can get messy!**
>
> ALM in Dataverse can become quite complex, and you can make it as hard as you want. But here, I'll show the basics of it for working with F&O.

Imagine you create a Power Automate flow that's complex enough that it took you several hours to create and get to work. You would usually do the development of this flow in a sandbox environment, and when it's done, move it to production, creating it from scratch. That would be quite time-consuming and inefficient.

Instead, what we would do is create a flow inside a solution, or add it to a solution (*see Figure 11.3*):

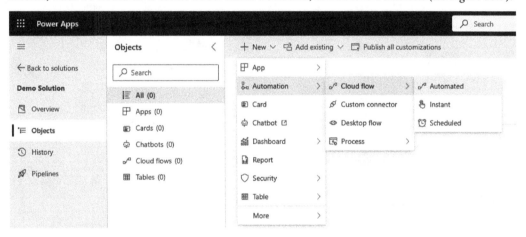

Figure 11.3 – Creating a new flow in a solution

Using the **New** button on the top menu of the solution screen, we can create the components we need, but if we've already created any component outside of a solution, we can add it to the solution using the **Add existing** option. We'll learn more about this later in the chapter. First, we need to learn about another tool that will help us with our ALM: publishers!

Publishers

Publishers serve several purposes in solutions for Power Platform. The first one is that any component created in a solution is owned by the publisher of that solution. This ensures that components created by others do not conflict with yours.

Each publisher has a different prefix, and this helps prevent duplicate component names. For example, if *Publisher A* has an `aas` prefix and *Publisher B* has an `xpp` prefix, and both create a flow named `HTTPTriggerCreate`, for *Publisher A*, it will be saved as `aas_httptriggercreate`, and for *Publisher B*, it will be `xpp_httptriggercreate`. Otherwise, they would have the same name, and we'd have a conflict when importing them to another environment.

All Power Platform environments have a default publisher, which has the new prefix. It's recommended to create a new publisher where your Power Platform components will be created. We can do that from the **New solution** dialog (see *Figure 11.4*):

New solution   ✕

Display name *

Name *

Publisher *

Select a Publisher   ⌄   🖉

\+ New publisher

Version *

1.0.0.0

More options ⌄

Figure 11.4 – Creating a new publisher

In the **New solution** dialog, just click on the **New publisher** button. This will open another dialog where we need to provide some details for the new publisher (see *Figure 11.5*):

Figure 11.5 – New publisher required fields

The display name, name, and description fields will later provide information about the publisher. The prefix will be the one used in your components, and the **Choice value prefix** field is generated automatically.

Environment variables

Another thing that will help us with our ALM and that is related to solutions is environment variables.

Using environment variables in our solutions will make changing fixed values (such as URLs) in our apps or flows faster when moving solutions between Dataverse environments. Let's see a quick example.

Create a **New solution**, and then click the **New** button, **More**, and **Environment variable** to create a new environment variable (see *Figure 11.6*):

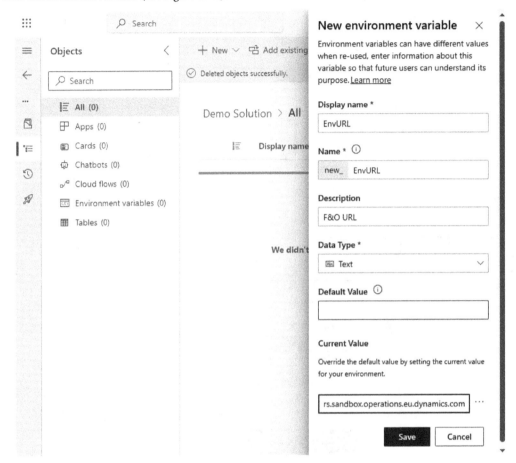

Figure 11.6 – Creating a new environment variable

Give the environment variable a name in the **Display name** field, a description, and change the **Data Type** value to **Text**, then click **New value** under **Current Value**, add your F&O environment URL, without the `https://` piece or the last `/` instance, and click the **Save** button. For example, if your F&O environment URL is `https://demo-fno.sandbox.operations.eu.dynamics.com/`, you just need to enter `demo-fno.sandbox.operations.eu.dynamics.com`.

If you use the same values as mine, this will create a `new_EnvURL` environment variable.

> **Power Platform publisher**
> Notice the `new_` prefix? As we've learned, that depends on the publisher you're using, and it could be a different prefix if the publisher you're using has been configured with a different prefix.

Now, create a new instant cloud flow within the solution. Add the **Get a record** action of the F&O connector (see *Figure 11.7*):

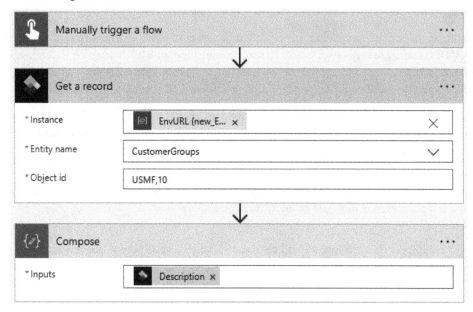

Figure 11.7 – Using the environment variable in a flow

In the **Instance** field, instead of selecting the environment URL as you would usually do, scroll down and select **Enter custom value**. This will open the **Dynamic content** window (see *Figure 11.8*):

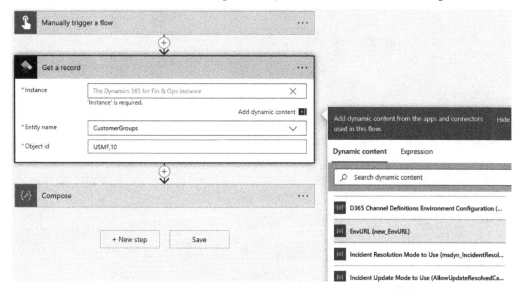

Figure 11.8 – Environment variable in the Dynamic content window

Scroll down to the environment variables until you find yours and select it. Then, for the example, select the `CustomerGroups` entity and select **Any**. Finally, add a **Compose** action where you will add the description returned by the **Get a record** action. Save it and test it.

After testing successfully in a sandbox environment, we want to move this flow to production. We could create it manually in Dataverse's production environment because it's a small flow. But remember – this is an example because I want to show you how to use environment variables, and if this were a huge flow, doing it by hand and changing all the environment URLs would take some time.

What we're going to do is this: first, we will edit the environment variable and remove its current value; then, we'll export the solution, change the production environment, and import the solution there.

> **Export and import**
>
> We will see all the details and options available to export and import solutions later in this chapter, but for now, you just need to know these operations exist.

Now, when we import the solution, we will get a screen where we can input the new environment URL (see *Figure 11.9*):

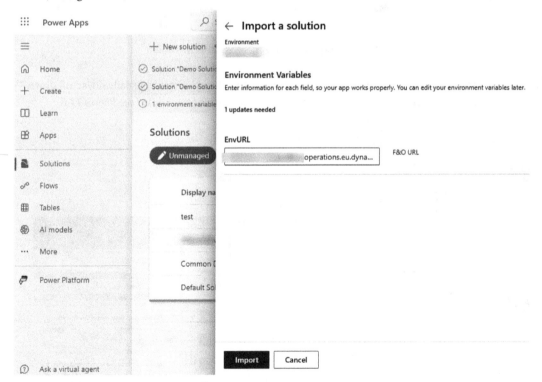

Figure 11.9 – Updating the value of the environment variable

In this step, we need to update the EnvURL variable we created with the URL of the new environment so that when we run the flow, it will use the updated URL.

Why are we deleting the value before exporting it? If we set a default value or current value and export that in the solution, it will be used in the environment where we import it, and we won't get the dialog asking for the new value.

We've learned a bit about solutions and environment variables; now, it's time to learn about managed and unmanaged solutions.

Managed and unmanaged solutions

Another important concept we need to learn about before working with solutions is managed and unmanaged solutions.

Unmanaged solutions are usually used during development while you're building your apps, flows, and so on. You can export an unmanaged solution as unmanaged or managed. Managed solutions are used to deploy to environments where no development for that specific solution is done; for example, a test or production environment.

If you export an unmanaged solution as unmanaged and import it into another environment, you will be able to edit its components. That involves opening the flow in the editor and changing how it behaves.

If you export a solution as managed and import it into another environment, you won't be able to edit any of the components in that solution. Beware! You could add any of the components to a new unmanaged solution and then you could edit them, but that would create a dependency between this new unmanaged solution and the original managed one, and if you wanted to uninstall the managed solution, you'd have to delete the unmanaged solution first.

We have two more important differences between managed and unmanaged solutions: the first one is that you can't export a managed solution from an environment. It's only possible to export unmanaged solutions. The second difference is that when you delete an unmanaged solution, its components are not deleted but added to the environment's default solution, while if you uninstall (delete) a managed solution, all its components will be deleted.

> **Managed versus unmanaged – fight!**
>
> You might've heard there are people who advocate for using managed solutions in specific scenarios and unmanaged in others different from the one I've covered here. However, in this section, I'll stick with what the official *Microsoft Learn* documentation recommends at the time of writing and leave this battle to people more experienced in the Dataverse field.

With this information, and me being a developer, it really makes sense to use unmanaged solutions for development and export them as managed to deploy to UAT, test, or production environments.

If you want, we can make a bit of parallelism, whereby a Dataverse-managed solution would be like a binary package in F&O, like the ones some ISVs use to distribute their products. We can install them in our environment, but we can't see the code. We can also compare this to how we deploy code in F&O: sandbox and production environments don't contain code, only binaries – exactly what I compared managed solutions to!

Unmanaged solutions would be the **Application Object Tree (AOT)** objects whose code we can see, edit, or extend in Visual Studio. And in this case, we do have code in the development environments, like unmanaged solutions in this comparison! I think we've got the most important concepts about solutions all lined up. In the next section, we'll learn about exporting and importing solutions.

Exporting and importing solutions

We've created an app; with its connections, it calls some flows and communicates with some different environments. We've tested that, and now we want to move it to a UAT environment where the users will test and learn.

Hopefully, the solution you've created in your dev environment is an unmanaged solution because of what we learned in the previous section. Let's see in more detail how we can export a solution and which options we have.

Publishing an unmanaged solution

Let me start with something we haven't talked about yet. When we export an unmanaged solution and we've made changes to it, we must publish it first. We can do this in the export functionality. After clicking the **Export** button, we get a dialog where we can choose to publish the changes before continuing with the export process (see *Figure 11.10*):

Figure 11.10 – Publishing all changes from the Export dialog

The other way is from the **Overview** screen in the solution (see *Figure 11.11*):

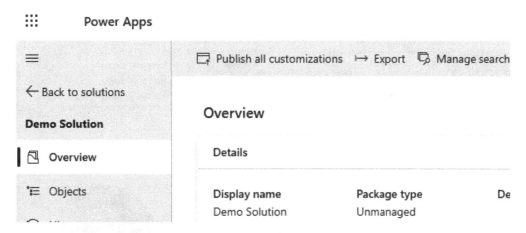

Figure 11.11 – Publishing from solution overview

Here, we can publish all changes before choosing to export the solution. Regardless of whether you publish changes from the export dialog or the main solution page, the process of publishing is the same from both places. What if you don't publish your changes? Some of its components may not be included in the exported solution.

Exporting a solution

Let me start this section by remembering that we can only export unmanaged solutions, so we'll stick to these in this part of the chapter.

For this, I've prepared an example of a solution that contains an environment variable of type text called EnvName and a canvas app that displays the value of that environment variable (see *Figure 11.12*):

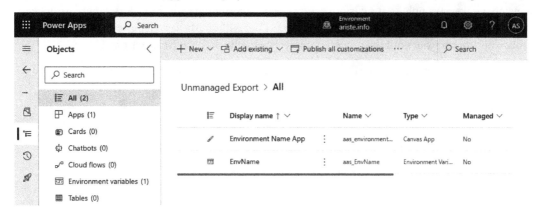

Figure 11.12 – Unmanaged solution contents

We can see both components in the **All** node. Now, go back to the solution overview, select it, and click the **Export** button to display the export dialog (see *Figure 11.13*):

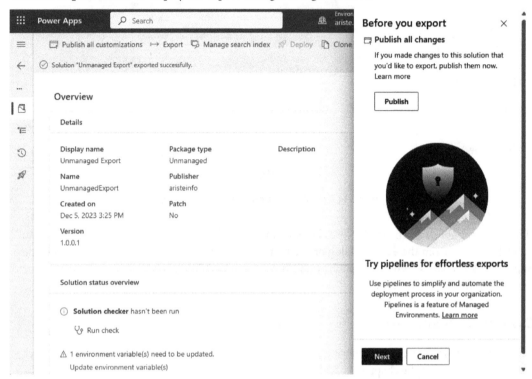

Figure 11.13 – Export dialog and Publish button

Remember – we must publish the customizations before continuing with the export; otherwise, when you import the solution, you will get the components but without the last changes done, so click the **Publish** button and wait until the process completes. Finally, click the **Next** button.

Now, we need to select between exporting the solution as managed or unmanaged (see *Figure 11.14*):

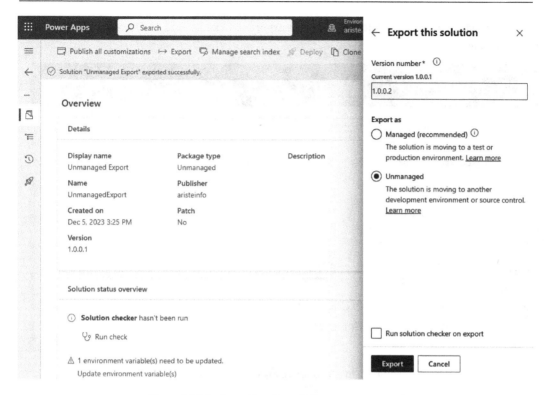

Figure 11.14 – Exporting the solution as unmanaged

For this example, we'll go with the **Unmanaged** solution. Notice the version number? Each time you export a solution, the version number is autoincremented on its last digit. Finally, click the **Export** button.

The dialog will close and a notification will appear at the top, just below the menu (see *Figure 11.15*):

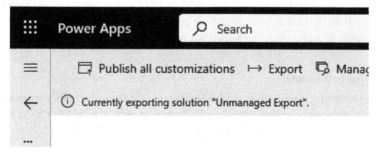

Figure 11.15: Solution being exported

The message will be displayed while the solution is exported. Once it's ready, a **Download** button will appear (see *Figure 11.16*):

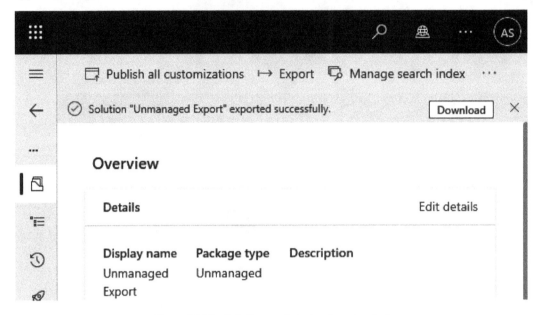

Figure 11.16 – Solution ready to be downloaded

When we click the **Download** button, we will get a ZIP file with our solution. And that's all. Now, let's see how we can import this solution into another environment.

Importing an unmanaged solution

Now that we have our unmanaged solution, we want to move the components we've created to another environment. We will do that using the ZIP file we got after exporting it in the previous step. Head to the target environment and go into the **Solutions** menu.

> **Importing is always the same!**
>
> The process of importing a solution is always the same regardless of whether we're importing a managed or an unmanaged solution. Click the **Import a solution** button on the top menu, and a dialog where we will upload the ZIP file will appear (see *Figure 11.17*).

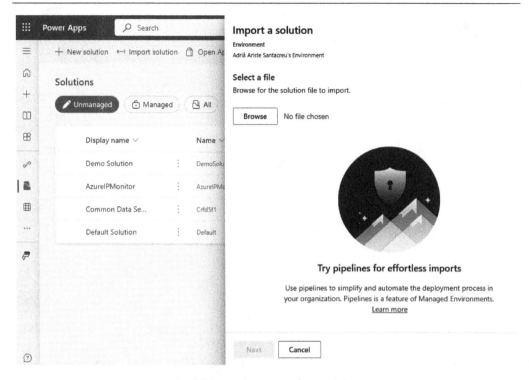

Figure 11.17 – Import a solution dialog

Note that the environment name is displayed at the top of the dialog. This is helpful so that we don't upload the solution to another environment by mistake. Click the **Browse** button and select your exported solution. Then, click the **Next** button.

The next screen of the dialog shows information on the solution: its name, publisher, version, or type. Click **Next** again, and it will ask you for the new value of the environment variable (see *Figure 11.18*):

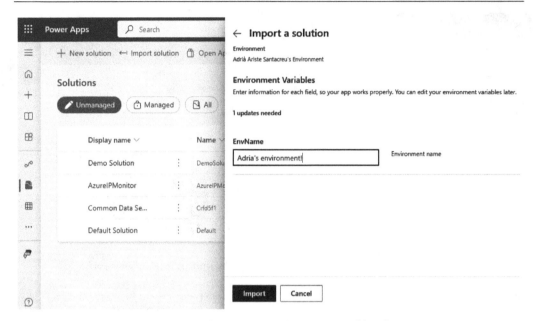

Figure 11.18 – Setting new environment variable value

Enter the new value, as we did in the *Environment variables* section before, and click the **Import** button. This will set the EnvName variable's value as Adria's environment!. The dialog will close, and a similar notification to the one we got when exporting the solution will appear (see *Figure 11.19*):

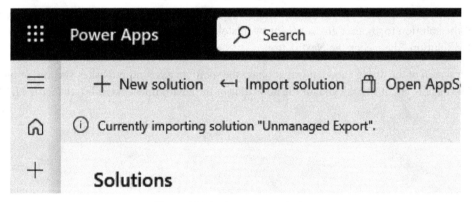

Figure 11.19 – Importing solution

The notification will stay under the top menu while the solution is being imported, and also, as in the export process, the message will change when done (see *Figure 11.20*):

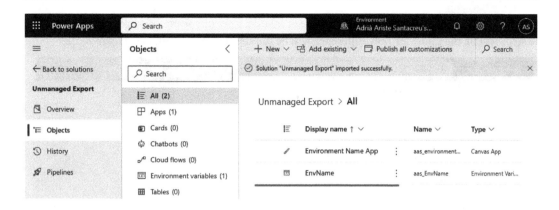

Figure 11.20 – Imported solution

The solution has been imported successfully, and we can see its components in the **Solution Explorer**. Let's run the app now and see if updating the environment variable value during the import process worked (see *Figure 11.21*):

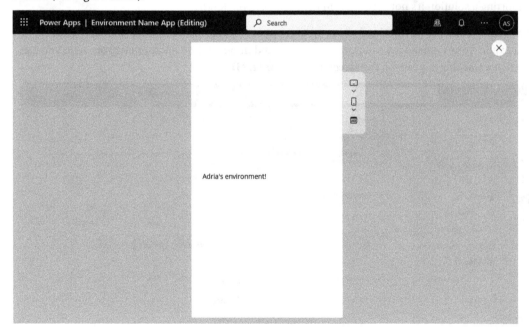

Figure 11.21 – Updated value in the app

We can see that the canvas app is displaying the value of the new text we entered when importing the solution.

This process will be the same regardless of the type of solution we're importing: managed or unmanaged. The steps will be the same; the only difference will be the solution placement (see *Figure 11.22*):

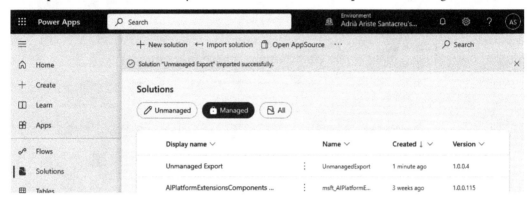

Figure 11.22 – Managed solutions filter

Managed solutions appear when the filter is set on **Managed** (or, obviously, **All**), so don't panic if after importing a solution it's not appearing in the list; check the filters!

And remember what we discussed about the components of managed solutions not being editable? If you export your unmanaged solution as managed and import it into another environment, you can see that a warning appears on the screen (see *Figure 11.23*):

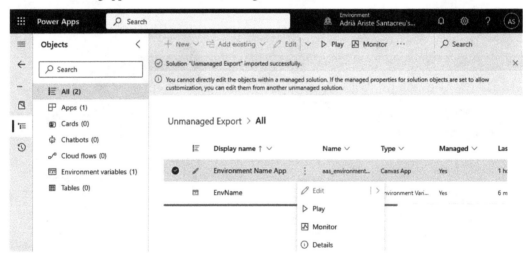

Figure 11.23 – Components in a managed solution

We will see a message warning us that we cannot edit the objects (components) inside of a managed solution. If we try to edit any of the components in the solution, we see the edit option is grayed out.

Now we know how we can create solutions, export them, and import them, we can move the components we create between environments.

Summary

In this chapter, we've delved into the significance and application of solutions in Power Platform. Solutions allow us to group components such as apps, flows, or tables in Power Platform. We've also learned a bit about what ALM is and how to manage the life of an application.

We've also learned about publishers in solutions, highlighting how they can prevent component conflicts and assist in organizing components efficiently. Also, we introduced the concept of environment variables, demonstrating how they simplify the task of modifying fixed values in apps or flows across different environments. We looked at the difference between managed and unmanaged solutions, with unmanaged solutions recommended for development and managed solutions recommended for deployment in non-development environments.

Finally, we've seen how to export and import solutions, and the importance of publishing changes before exporting anything. This section is key to understanding how to efficiently manage and move Power Platform components between different stages of development and deployment.

With this chapter, we've reached the end of the book, in which we've focused on low-code tools in Power Platform to solve scenarios in Dynamics 365 F&O. We've explored various components such as Power Apps, Power Automate, Power BI, and AI Builder, explaining their integration and application in enhancing F&O functionalities.

We've discussed concepts such as Dual-write, virtual tables, and Dataverse, emphasizing their role in data integration and synchronization, and addressed practical scenarios and implementation examples, offering a way to use Power Platform to speed up our F&O implementations.

Moving forward, let me emphasize one last time the importance of embracing low-code tools for faster, more efficient customization and development. I encourage all of you to continue exploring the capabilities of Power Platform, particularly its potential to innovate and transform business processes in Dynamics 365 F&O environments.

Questions

Now, it's time to test your solution knowledge with these questions:

1. What is the primary purpose of using solutions in Power Platform?

    a. To provide automated data backup

    b. To group components such as apps, flows, or tables

    c. To enhance the graphical user interface

    d. To increase the processing speed of applications

2. What does ALM stand for in the context of Power Platform development?

   a. Automatic lifecycle management

   b. Application lifecycle management

   c. Advanced logic mechanism

   d. Agile learning methodology

3. Why are environment variables used in Power Platform solutions?

   a. To increase the security of data stored in solutions

   b. To track the version history of each component

   c. To simplify modifying fixed values such as URLs when moving solutions between environments

   d. To automatically translate app content based on user location

4. What distinguishes a managed solution from an unmanaged solution in Power Platform?

   a. Managed solutions are editable, whereas unmanaged solutions are not

   b. Managed solutions are used for development, while unmanaged solutions are used for deployment

   c. Unmanaged solutions can be exported and edited, but managed solutions cannot

   d. Unmanaged solutions are for data analysis, whereas managed solutions are for data storage

5. What is the role of publishers in the context of Power Platform solutions?

   a. They provide financial support for app development

   b. They ensure components created do not conflict with each other

   c. They are responsible for marketing the solutions.

   d. They automatically update the Power Platform software

Further reading

To learn more about the topics covered in this chapter, you can visit the following links:

Overview of application lifecycle management with Microsoft Power Platform: `https://learn.microsoft.com/en-us/power-platform/alm/overview-alm`

Solution concepts: `https://learn.microsoft.com/en-us/power-platform/alm/solution-concepts-alm`

Managed and unmanaged solutions: `https://learn.microsoft.com/en-us/ power-platform/alm/solution-concepts-alm#managed-and-unmanaged- solutions`

Environment variables overview: `https://learn.microsoft.com/en-us/power- apps/maker/data-platform/environmentvariables`

Answers

1. b. To group components such as apps, flows, or tables
2. b. Application lifecycle management
3. c. To simplify modifying fixed values such as URLs when moving solutions between environments
4. c. Unmanaged solutions can be exported and edited, but managed solutions cannot
5. b. They ensure components created do not conflict with each other

Index

Packtpub.com

Subscribe to our online digital library for full access to over 7,000 books and videos, as well as industry leading tools to help you plan your personal development and advance your career. For more information, please visit our website.

Why subscribe?

- Spend less time learning and more time coding with practical eBooks and Videos from over 4,000 industry professionals

- Improve your learning with Skill Plans built especially for you

- Get a free eBook or video every month

- Fully searchable for easy access to vital information

- Copy and paste, print, and bookmark content

Did you know that Packt offers eBook versions of every book published, with PDF and ePub files available? You can upgrade to the eBook version at packtpub.com and as a print book customer, you are entitled to a discount on the eBook copy. Get in touch with us at customercare@packtpub.com for more details.

At www.packtpub.com, you can also read a collection of free technical articles, sign up for a range of free newsletters, and receive exclusive discounts and offers on Packt books and eBooks.

Other Books You May Enjoy

If you enjoyed this book, you may be interested in these other books by Packt:

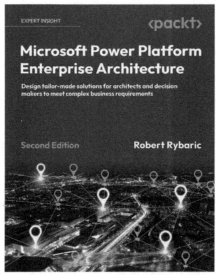

Microsoft Power Platform Enterprise Architecture - Second Edition

Robert Rybaric

ISBN: 978-1-80461-263-7

- Understand various Microsoft Dynamics 365 CRM, ERP, and AI modules for creating Power Platform solutions
- Combine Power Platform capabilities with Microsoft 365 and Azure
- Find out which regions, staging environments, and user licensing groups need to be employed when creating enterprise solutions
- Implement sophisticated security by using various authentication and authorization techniques
- Extend Microsoft Power BI, Power Apps, and Power Automate to create custom applications
- Integrate your solution with various in-house Microsoft components or third-party systems using integration patterns
- Migrate data using a variety of approaches and best practices

Extending Microsoft Business Central with Power Platform

Kim Congleton, Shawn Sissenwein

ISBN: 978-1-80324-071-8

- Build and deploy robust Power Platform solutions for Business Central
- Seamlessly integrate Business Central both in the cloud and on-premises with Power Platform using a wide range of connectors
- Set up virtual tables and gain insights into the extensive capabilities of Dataverse
- Build and connect Power Apps, enabling seamless Power BI integration for Business Central
- Create exceptional automated flows with advanced Power Automate configurations
- Understand user adoption strategies and the center of excellence

Packt is searching for authors like you

If you're interested in becoming an author for Packt, please visit `authors.packtpub.com` and apply today. We have worked with thousands of developers and tech professionals, just like you, to help them share their insight with the global tech community. You can make a general application, apply for a specific hot topic that we are recruiting an author for, or submit your own idea.

Share Your Thoughts

Now you've finished *Extending Dynamics 365 Finance and Operations Apps with Power Platform*, we'd love to hear your thoughts! Scan the QR code below to go straight to the Amazon review page for this book and share your feedback or leave a review on the site that you purchased it from.

`https://packt.link/r/1-801-81159-8`

Your review is important to us and the tech community and will help us make sure we're delivering excellent quality content.

Download a free PDF copy of this book

Thanks for purchasing this book!

Do you like to read on the go but are unable to carry your print books everywhere?

Is your eBook purchase not compatible with the device of your choice?

Don't worry, now with every Packt book you get a DRM-free PDF version of that book at no cost.

Read anywhere, any place, on any device. Search, copy, and paste code from your favorite technical books directly into your application.

The perks don't stop there, you can get exclusive access to discounts, newsletters, and great free content in your inbox daily

Follow these simple steps to get the benefits:

1. Scan the QR code or visit the link below

https://packt.link/free-ebook/9781801811590

2. Submit your proof of purchase
3. That's it! We'll send your free PDF and other benefits to your email directly